Save Our Children

The Struggle Between Black Families and Schools

Dr. Twyla J. Williams

First Edition, First Printing

Front cover illustration by Harold Carr, Jr.

Copyright © 2009 by Dr. Twyla J. Williams

Printed in the United States of America

10-Digit ISBN #: 1-934155-16-0
13-Digit ISBN #: 978-1-934155-16-5

This book is dedicated to my grandparents, Clarence E. Hamilton, Sr. (deceased) and his beautiful bride, Minnie Hamilton.

Contents

Acknowledgements

To God be the glory! I am forever grateful for His grace and mercy that has allowed me to share the voices of middle-class African American parents in this our noble quest: to make education equitable for all children.

I appreciate every family who participated in my study. Without your narratives, this project would not exist.

Dr. Jawanza Kunjufu and African American Images, I appreciate you for giving me this opportunity to publish.

I would like to thank Margaree Mitchell, MKM Book Services Company, for converting a dissertation and an idea into a manuscript.

To Dr. Norvella Carter, my professor, mentor, scholarly mother, and Grand Woman of God, thank you for teaching me how to move beyond my own limits. You have overcome unimaginable obstacles, and many lives have been enriched because of your "enduring hardness as a good soldier!"

Thanks to my parents FD and Jean Quiller for always believing in me and praying for me. Thank you for your endless sacrifices. I am who I am because of you and your love.

Destiny and Noah, you are the greatest! Thank you for your understanding and support while Mom took time to complete this book. Your question, "Are you done yet?" motivated me to keep going.

I must refrain from listing more names as it would require a second book, so to *ALL* my family and friends who served as supporters, critics, motivators, cheerleaders, and babysitters, I thank and love you all! It has truly taken a village for me to complete this project. I want you all to know that I could not have accomplished this project without you!

Save Our Children
The Struggle between Black Families and Schools

Foreword

When I was a child in the 1950's, it was clearly communicated to us as Blacks and African Americans that education was the key to a quality life and the survival of future generations. It was communicated that we were not yet equal to European Americans because we were subjected to an inferior educational system. Our struggles had nothing to do with racism but with our need to be educated. Of course this mindset has always been a lie among many lies to cover the monstrous evil of racism that has been at the foundational core of our nation since its inception. Today, through the sacrifices of parents, educators, civil rights and community leaders, there are millions of educated African Americans. Yet, the struggle to educate our children en mass has not changed. Poor and middle-class African Americans share the same fight: to successfully educate their children.

Dr. Twyla Williams elaborates on this struggle by describing how educated African American parents are treated in so-called "exemplary" educational settings that are predominately European American, middle-class, and suburban. Dr. Williams chose to concentrate on this particular group to dispel some of the myths around getting our children into "good" schools for the purpose of a quality education. Her selection was strategic because it demonstrates that we as a people still struggle, even when educational and financial support are present. These parents provided their children with school preparation, involvement, and financial support. Interestingly, these are the factors that are usually cited as lacking among Black students who fail in poverty stricken schools. If African American students do not suffer from societal ills that are so-called "culprits of academic success," then why do they struggle in school?

According to Dr. Williams, the public school system flagrantly contributes to the academic struggles of our children. In this text, the author describes, with scholarly research, how our children are segregated within integrated schools, systematically discriminated against, and subjected to hegemonic practices. Hegemony is a term that refers to those who are led to participate in their own oppression. The author gives a vivid picture of how tracking and grouping enter the lives of our children early on, relegating them to low level instruction and sometimes unwarranted special education. As African American parents, we are aware of the overrepresentation of our children in special education and their underrepresentation in honors and advanced placement classes. Dr. Williams gives voice to this lament. Not since Ellis Cose's book, *The Rage of a Privileged Class: Why Do Prosperous Blacks Still Have the Blues?* has an author provided such a descriptive view.

Dr. Williams' poignant chapter on the school system's role in the struggle is followed by a riveting description of educators, particularly European Americans, who prohibit the success of our children in school. She cites too many teachers as having a low sense of teacher efficacy, which is the extent to which teachers believe they can really teach the children and make a difference in their lives. Dr. Williams promotes the need for teachers to be prepared to teach all children in this diverse society. With the majority of teachers in this nation being European American, middle-class females who have not received the preparation necessary to teach all children, a definite challenge exists. The author also considers the notion of privilege. Should all children have the opportunity to be "the best?"

The case study that Dr. Williams shares is most revealing. She studied the perceptions of African American mothers and what they thought about the interactions that occurred between their children and predominately European American teachers in suburban junior high classrooms in three schools. She provides a rich description by using the actual words of the mothers. The findings of her study are profound because her work shares the lived experiences of these mothers.

Often readers will encounter the works of writers who tell gripping stories that end in despair and hopelessness. Although many of the experiences of the parents are painful, Dr. Williams does not leave the reader hanging in despair. One of the characteristics of an empowering educator is his or her ability to inspire hope for the future. Readers of this work will be able to reflect on its contents and conclude that it gives voice to parents and children who are oppressed by our educational system. In addition, Dr. Williams provides insights on the lessons parents learned in her study. She stresses the pursuit of high achievement in the midst of struggle and provides strategic solutions for educating African American children. She should be applauded for this insightful work. It will be beneficial to parents, educators, political leaders, and anyone interested in the education of African American students.

Norvella Carter, Ph.D.
Endowed Chair in Urban Education
Texas A&M University

Introduction: Why We Must Save *All* Our Children

Destiny, my daughter, is a very bright girl. During her preschool years, Destiny learned to read, speak conversational Spanish, and quote Bible verses from memory. Academically Destiny excelled and her communication skills were exceptional among her peers. She was a confident child and would start a conversation with anyone willing to listen. Destiny has always had a passion for music. She sings and dances at church and community gatherings.

Today Destiny is nine years old and is in the third grade. She attends a school in a predominately White suburban school district. Her experiences in the district have been challenging at times, and they stirred within me a desire to change conditions for African American students in suburban schools. Because of my own experiences with Destiny in kindergarten and beyond, I was able to relate to other mothers who experienced similar challenges.

Upon entering kindergarten, Destiny was extremely excited and eager to learn. She is a logical child who excels at solving problems in difficult situations. However, after a few weeks of school, she came home disappointed because her classmates were only learning one letter of the alphabet each week. I was extremely disappointed and felt that Destiny's gifts were not being developed.

Destiny soon became bored and lost interest in school. She complained of stomach aches and did not want to go. That served as a red flag to me. My daughter was not enjoying what should have been a fun and stimulating rite of passage into public education. My husband and I toiled with the decision to have her tested to accelerate her to first grade.

Kindergarten is a critical year, and we did not want to rush her.

We scheduled a meeting with her teacher. Before the meeting, the teacher had Destiny take a sample section of the standardized test so we could discuss the results when we met.

The test results showed that Destiny was advanced. The teacher was impressed but not sure Destiny tested high enough to be successful in first grade. She was also reluctant to recommend Destiny for first grade because of her unfamiliarity with some of the language used on the exams (e.g., "uppercase letters" versus "capital letters"). Were White children being accelerated to first grade based on being able to read certain words, or was it the school's policy to keep all children in kindergarten? I suspected that technicalities and not a lack of ability would prevent Destiny from going to first grade early.

The teacher encouraged us to be patient. She said that by the end of the year, all children in the class would be at the same level. Did this teacher even believe that Destiny was capable of excelling? She certainly seemed to have low expectations of my child. Did she expect Destiny to conform to her low expectations?

My husband and I did not push the issue. We decided to let Destiny remain in kindergarten. Unfortunately, as the year progressed, Destiny displayed behavioral problems that caused us to reconsider our decision. We received notes and phone calls complaining about Destiny talking to other students during quiet time and on the "red carpet." The red carpet was the area in the classroom where students were expected to sit quietly.

Introduction: Why We Must Save
All Our Children

Clearly my child was bored, but because we value education, we insisted that she conform and obey the rules. Privately I wondered if Destiny was the only student with these issues. Perhaps the teacher needed help with classroom management.

Despite Destiny's behavior, the teacher recognized her potential. In addition to her regular class work, Destiny was given several duties to perform. From the first day of school, Destiny was the teacher's helper. She assisted students who had learning difficulties. She tutored students who sat at her table, and she was a "special friend" to a student who was experiencing separation anxiety from her mother. We did not send our child to school to be a teacher's aide. We wanted her to interact with her peers at her own level and to excel in reading, math, and other academic subjects.

Destiny's behavioral problems may have been caused by the teacher's special treatment of her. We think Destiny felt that the rules did not apply to her because of the responsibilities she had been given. We became concerned and decided to have her screened for the gifted and talented program.

There were five components to the screening. After completion of the first two components, Destiny advanced to the remaining components. Although her scores on parts of the screening were exceptional, she did not qualify. She needed to have positive marks in four of the five components and was exceptional in only three. I contacted the gifted and talented specialist for further explanation concerning Destiny's score, but none was given.

Many questions came to mind. Had the teacher intervened? Were special considerations ever given to White children who qualified in only three areas? How many African

American students were in the gifted and talented program? Did other African American parents have this problem? I felt disappointed with the school system. I knew Destiny was exceptionally bright and had many gifted and talented characteristics. Destiny's teacher also believed she was extremely bright based on the checklist she completed but apparently not bright enough for the educational system to recognize her abilities. Instead of fighting the decision, we decided to provide supplemental enrichment through community and church activities.

This was my first experience in a suburban school district with middle-income White teachers. Like most parents, we have high expectations of our child, which is why we enrolled her in a high performing school district with a strong reputation. Having encountered numerous difficulties and frustrations from the beginning of Destiny's education, however, we began to reconsider the school district we chose for her. Did we make the right decision? Would Destiny receive the best education possible to be successful in life? Would she embrace her race and heritage in a positive light?

We regrouped and decided to do whatever we could to support our child academically and emotionally. We decided to have lunch with her at school throughout the year, enrich her reading experiences at home, and cultivate a love for learning through the supplemental activities.

The lunch visits were very enlightening. During one particular visit, I witnessed how students were disciplined differently based on their race. A little White girl broke a cafeteria rule. The monitor very nicely said, "Please do not break the rule." Then he gave the girl a friendly pat on her hand. A few minutes later, an African American boy broke the same rule. The monitor walked over to him, reprimanded him harshly in front of his peers, and ordered him to take his lunch tray to an isolated area. I watched quietly to see if the other adults in the cafeteria would address the action, but they did not. I asked an African American custodian if she saw what happened. She said what I witnessed occurred on a regular basis. I asked her if she had ever talked to the administrators at the school about this problem. She said she had not shared this information with anyone. I encouraged her to do so. I also asked the monitor why he treated the students differently when they had broken the same rule. He refused to give me an answer.

As I sat across from my Destiny, I realized that at some point she might have experienced this kind of treatment, and I felt very sad. I was concerned for the students of color at Destiny's school and in the district. They deserved better treatment. I began to think about how race plays out in public schools. I wondered about the covert and overt discrimination that occurred every day at schools across the country. At that moment, I knew in my heart that the voices of middle-income African American parents with children in suburban schools *must* be heard, and I would begin with the mothers. I would ask them about their children's school experiences in predominately White suburban junior high schools and their own interactions with their children's White teachers.

Case Study Approach

Storytelling organically leads to the development of case studies. The stories presented in this book lend a human voice to the data that has emerged in other studies. Clearly more research is needed to truly understand the experiences of African American students in affluent, predominately White schools, but the case study presented in this book is a good start. The case study opens a window into the lives of Black families who are attempting to negotiate the minefield of race and education in White schools. Their challenges and successes can help all African American parents, regardless of income and can also improve their children's classroom experience.

Black parents have always taught their children that the way to a better life is through education. The way to combat racial discrimination and achieve equality in American society is through a *good* education. Many families believe this and have attempted to prepare their children for the future by insisting that they excel in school.

In the decades following the civil rights movement, the Black middle class began to grow. These families sought the best education they could find for their children, believing that the better the education, the more opportunities their children would have in life. As a result, there has been an exodus to more affluent communities because the schools tend to be "better" there. The general belief seems to be, "If our children attend these high achieving schools, no barriers can hold them back."

My experience with Destiny caused me to reconsider these basic assumptions. I decided to investigate the experiences of other families. Were our children being nurtured in suburban schools as their ancestors had been in segregated Black schools? Did the teachers respect their race, culture, and heritage? Were African American students being encouraged to be all they could be even though they were the minority in these schools? Was the suburban school environment healthy and positive for African American students?

Introduction: Why We Must Save
All Our Children

What about our students' self-esteem? Did they feel a sense of belonging to the school community? Were they being encouraged to believe that the sky was the limit? These questions and more swirled around in my mind.

My decision to investigate how Black mothers viewed their interactions with White teachers was based on the need to understand the many problems Black students face in affluent, predominately White schools. This book will allow their voices to be heard, as well as allow them to advocate for their children.

Six African American mothers participated in this study in 2006. They identified themselves as middle income. Their families live in suburban communities, and their children are zoned to their neighborhood schools (versus being bussed from other areas). For the purpose of this study, suburb is defined as a family-oriented, predominately White community. Parents are college-educated, middle-income professionals, and the minimum value of homes is $140,000. The average annual salary of the families participating in the study is $200,000.

I wanted to focus on the families' approach to high stakes education, so I narrowed the participant pool to include only mothers who fought to enroll their children in advanced placement courses. Perhaps no program prepares students for college more than advanced placement. The mothers in the study believed that taking advanced placement courses was critical to their children's academic success.

My approach to understanding the experiences of the participants is *interpretivism,* or the making of meaning through interpretation. Using the participants' stories, I have fashioned a case study that explains the process of how and why events occurred. Case studies are perfect for an interpretivistic approach because they allow for a certain subjectivity and freedom when interviewing participants. The case study presented in this book truly represents, to the best of my ability, the voices of African American mothers who have undergone a unique experience in America, one that is little known, barely appreciated, and definitely misunderstood.

Both individual and group interviews were conducted in the homes of the participants. Group sessions were freewheeling, often mirroring the communication style of traditional Black churches. For example, one participant would begin to share, and then another would speak while the other mothers nodded and verbally affirmed their agreement. There was much waving of hands and even "Amens!" Not only did I capture and analyze these heartfelt expressions, their testimonies were a witness to the stunning commonality of experience that African American families in the suburbs share. This was a revelation because African Americans are so few in number in affluent communities and are often spread out geographically. However, our sessions revealed to us all that we were not alone after all.

Critical Lens Focused on Race

This study unapologetically focuses on race—African American families and their White teachers. This approach was influenced by critical race theory, i.e., racism is "normal," not abnormal in American society, and it is intertwined in the fabric of the social order. Critical race theory in education looks at the perspectives, methods, and pedagogy of educators in order to identify, analyze, and transform the structural, cultural, and interpersonal aspects of schools that marginalize students of color.

Storytelling has also been incorporated into critical race theory. Storytelling is a method that uses reflections and life stories to build theories about the nature of race and racism. In this study, the mothers' stories add depth and dimension to our understanding of how race and racism influence students' school experiences.

Applying critical race theory to education enables us to investigate and analyze how many White educators assume normative standards of "Whiteness" in the classroom and how these values, attitudes, and behaviors impact the development and academic achievement of African American students. Critical race theory in education seeks to uncover the history of racial subordination and the "color blind" perspective often demonstrated by White teachers in the classroom. Through narratives and historical evidence, critical race theory documents the racial isolation (both imposed and self-generated) of African American students and the ways some have had to compromise their racial identity to survive.

I attempted to understand the phenomenon from the participants' perspective. In the individual and group interviews, I took field notes, audio taped the sessions, and conducted member checks throughout the study.

Background of the District

Three junior high schools in the southeastern part of the United States were chosen for the study. They are located on the south side of a major interstate and are part of a large suburban school district (181 square miles and more than 40,000 students). The demographics of the student population in the district are as follows: 6.7 percent African American, 22.1 percent Hispanic, 63.5 percent White, 0.2 percent Native American, and 7.5 percent Asian/Pacific Islander. Teacher demographics are as follows: 2.7 percent African American, 5.7 percent Hispanic, 90.7 percent White, 0.2 percent Native American, and 0.6 percent Asian/Pacific Islander.

Purposive Sample

The six middle-income African American mothers were chosen by the purposive method of "snowball sampling." This involved asking African American mothers to recommend other African American mothers to participate in the study. The assumption was that the mothers would refer others who also had children in one of the three selected junior high schools.

I interviewed interested mothers by telephone to determine if they met the following criteria:
1. They lived in a suburban community within the attendance zone of the district.
2. They had at least one student attending or who once attended one of the three junior high schools selected for this study.
3. They self-identified as middle-income and African American.
4. Teachers recommended that students exit at least one advanced placement course in junior high school.

Upon qualifying, the mothers were invited to participate and asked to refer names and contact information of other mothers who might be interested in participating.

Data Collection

After the preliminary phone interviews, each mother participated in two one-hour semi-structured interviews. The first interview was used to obtain basic descriptive information about the participants, establish expectations and procedures, confirm the race of their children's teachers, establish rapport, and share some of their children's general experiences. Participants were asked to discuss their own educational and professional backgrounds as well as their children's personalities, honors and awards received, academic achievements, relationships with peers, and how they prepared their children for academic and social success. The mothers talked about their children's classroom experiences. Finally I asked them to provide the names and contact information of other mothers who might be interested in participating in the study. The second interview for some participants immediately followed the first, while other participants were rescheduled for a later date.

The second interview began with the participants continuing their narratives. I asked them more specific, guided questions about interactions between their children and their White teachers. All interviews were audio taped and transcribed. I also wrote field notes to document the observations and key words spoken during the interviews. As the mothers talked about their experiences, I noted the collage of emotions they displayed, ranging from happiness to outrage. These emotions were expressed through humor, sarcasm, and even trembling voices with tearful eyes. It was during those tearful times that I felt an enormous obligation to "fix" their problems.

The individual interviews were analyzed to look for emerging themes to guide the two group sessions (two hours each) that followed. It was important to bring the participants together to further explore the information given and to continue collecting experiential details. In addition, I wanted to verify, through member checks, that the emerging themes did indeed reflect the perceptions of the participants. Member checks in qualitative research allow the participants to affirm what the researcher has written to help improve the accuracy, credibility, and validity of the research.

Data Analysis

The data were collected and analyzed at the same time using the constant comparative method. I began with a particular incident from an interview and using my field notes, compared it with another incident in the same set of data or in another set. After the first set of individual interviews were audio taped and transcribed, the transcriptions and field notes were reviewed and analyzed. Key words and phrases were highlighted to further guide the research. Comparisons between the first and second set of interviews were made.

By constantly comparing the individual interviews, words and phrases were coded, and themes emerged. These themes guided the group sessions.

Member checks and themes enabled the participants to verify their perceptions of reality during the group sessions. Each theme would be discussed one at a time following a well-organized format—at least that was the original intention. Instead, the themes were intertwined as participants discussed their experiences. For example, one participant would begin to talk while another would continue her narrative. The names of the children were different, but the stories were often similar.

Without a doubt, race formed the centerpiece of this study. It emerged as the dominant theme that characterized students' interactions with their White teachers.

Introduction: Why We Must Save
All Our Children

Trustworthiness and Credibility

Throughout the process of data collection and analysis, intentional methods were employed to authenticate trustworthiness and credibility of this study. One method was prolonged engagement of four to six months with the participants. It was important for me to spend enough time with the participants so I could eliminate distortions and understand events from their perspective. Member checks of the individual transcripts ensured an accurate understanding of the mothers' perceptions. Given the different experiences and perspectives of the mothers, it was important to triangulate (use of more than one method) to articulate the mothers' points of view. Transcriptions and field notes from individual interviews and group sessions were triangulated.

Positionality

As the primary researcher for this study, it is important for me to state my position. I am a middle-income African American mother with a child in elementary school. I am currently employed as a junior high counselor in a predominately White suburban school.

As a counselor, I often talk to African American parents about the difficulties their children face with racism, isolation, and identity confusion. This has fueled my desire to report the concerns of middle-income African American parents.

My position enables me to serve as an advocate for African American families as well as the school in which I work. I must admit that it has been an extremely challenging position as I have to constantly assess and reassess where my true loyalties lie. I have listened to the concerns of African American parents and students as well as White teachers and administrators. While both sides have their points, my loyalties will always lie with our children.

It was difficult, but as a researcher I tried not to impose my views on any of the participants. I tried to be as objective as possible. That was most challenging when, during the interviews, parents made points that I could identify with as an African American and a mother. However, also understanding the educators' perspectives enabled me to stay balanced in my approach.

My prayer is that the case study presented in this book will provide more understanding about the needs of African Americans in affluent White schools and the challenges they face. I pray that parents will know better how to help their children and that suburban school districts will finally begin to deliver on their promise to provide a quality education for *all* students, regardless of their color.

Chapter 1: Education and the Black Family

All parents desire a quality education for their children. Whether Black or White, rich or poor, all children deserve highly qualified teachers, an intellectually stimulating curriculum, a racially tolerant school culture, safe school buildings, and equitable financing to make it all happen. We are well aware, however, that inequities do exist in the system and that children of poverty and children of color suffer the most from inferior schooling. It has been argued that poverty is a risk factor in academic performance, but as we will see throughout this work, middle-income students suffer in the classroom as well. As the following statistics so dramatically illustrate, the so-called academic achievement gap between Black and White students is a national disgrace.

- In 2005, only 55 percent of all Black students graduated from high school on time with a regular diploma, compared to 78 percent of Whites.
- In 2005, the on-time graduation rate for Black males was 48 percent nationally; for White males it was 74 percent.
- Nearly half of the nation's African American students, but only 11 percent of White students, attend high schools in which graduation is not the norm.
- In 2002, only 23 percent of all Black students who started public high school left prepared for college, compared to 40 percent of Whites.
- On average, African American and Hispanic students in 12th grade read at approximately the same level as White 8th graders.
- About half of poor, urban 9th graders read at only a 5th or 6th grade level.

- The National Assessment of Educational Progress reports that 88 percent of African American 8th graders read below grade level, compared to 62 percent of White 8th graders.
- The 12th grade reading scores of African American males were significantly lower than those for males and females across every other racial and ethnic group.

Parental Involvement

There is a strong correlation between children's academic achievement and parental involvement. Although the most effective level of involvement has not yet been determined, parents are still expected to be involved in their children's academic lives.

Parents are involved for different reasons and at different levels. Some initiate contact with teachers to check on their children's classroom progress. Some are active in the school's PTA/PTO. They chaperone field trips and volunteer in the classroom. Other parents only visit when poor academic performance or discipline issues arise. These parents are not likely to make spontaneous visits to the school.

Parents become involved because they want their children to succeed in school, but we should not assume that parents who are not as involved are no less concerned. Work schedules, among other things, factor into a parent's involvement level.

Parental involvement is an important issue in Black families. It is associated with improved attendance and classroom behavior, higher test scores, improved grades, drop out reduction, homework completion, and preparedness for college.

Parental involvement goes beyond participating in school activities. While schools are focused on education, parents are concerned about the overall well-being of their children. They view school success in the context of family and community support and their children's overall development. Quality relationships, emotional and spiritual health, and the development of life skills are as important as academic success.

While African American parents place a high value on education, they also value their children's involvement in church, recreation centers, etc. Parents, as managers of the home environment, encourage, organize, and supervise their children's educational opportunities in the home and broader community.

Parents are their children's best teachers and advocates when it comes to dealing with racial issues in school. In the *Journal of Marriage and Family,* Hughes and Johnson state:

> "Over the past several years, researchers have become increasingly interested in how parents shape children's learning about their own race and about relations between ethnic groups. Commonly referred to as racial socialization, parents' race-related communications to children have been viewed as important determinants of children's race related attitudes and beliefs and of their sense of efficacy in negotiating race-related barriers and experiences."

African American parents use race-related experiences to transmit cultural information, wisdom, and strategies for dealing with discrimination and injustice. These experiences also provide opportunities to help their children develop racial pride and self-esteem, strengths they'll need when attending predominately White suburban schools where cultural values differ from their own.

African American students in suburban schools are faced with challenges on a daily basis. Parents find they must invest time and energy, above and beyond academics and normal developmental issues, to prepare their children to deal with negative race-related experiences. When it comes to raising Black students in the suburbs, Hughes and Johnson claim that the racial socialization of parents is critical in influencing their children's identity development and well-being.

If students have self-esteem and a good sense of who they are, they are likely to be productive in school. Parents should feel empowered to know that despite the challenges, they can help their children succeed in school and develop a positive outlook.

Similar to the struggle for racial equality in the early decades of the 20th century, African Americans continue to seek equal access to quality schooling for their children. The fact that inner city schools have, by and large, failed our children has led many Black families to move to the suburbs where the schools enjoy a reputation of excellence.

However, those left behind are at times academically paralyzed and victimized by the idea that poverty is an obstacle to academic achievement. While poverty does create a myriad of social problems, it does not have to lead to poor classroom performance. There are many examples of student success in underserved schools. Parents are a child's best hope for academic success. Parents make the difference.

4

Parents may feel that because they are not as educated as their children's teachers, they cannot offer useful suggestions or help with homework. These parents create a division of labor between themselves and teachers. They do not want to interfere nor do they feel qualified to engage in classroom activities. So they stick with what they know: they enforce appropriate behaviors and motivate their children to do their best in school. This division of labor causes parents to feel a sense of powerlessness in their ability to improve the quality of their children's education. Researchers suggest that parents (especially, perhaps, low-income parents) are reluctant to talk to their children's teachers for fear of being judged as inadequate.

In the inner city, the parent-teacher partnership is tenuous at best. Parents depend on educators to serve as advocates for their children and to keep their children's best interests at heart. Whether in the city or suburbs, they are often overwhelmed by how much they are expected to contribute to their children's learning. In the suburbs where high parental involvement is expected (and tends to be the norm), the schools may provide little guidance. When it comes to the education of their children, African American parents are willing to challenge the status quo if they perceive that all is not right in the classroom and school overall. This aggressive advocacy may translate as an unwillingness to cooperate with teachers and administrators. African American parents are often seen as "difficult" in the suburbs.

Although it sometimes appears that the educational system does not value parents, they are indeed a critical factor in improving academic performance. Parents can provide intimate details about their children, information that cannot be obtained from tests. They know the strengths and weaknesses of their children.

Parents can become more effective advocates for their children by questioning and not simply accepting the word of teachers and administrators as law. Parents have a say. Parents have an important role. Whether low- or middle-income, whether your children are enrolled in schools in the city or suburbs, whether you have a college degree or not, you must advocate for your child. If something doesn't feel right, respectfully challenge it.

Middle-Income African American Families

Many African American parents base their decision to move to certain suburban areas solely on the reputation of the schools. They seek information that will help them choose the school that offers the best educational advantages for their children. The school environment must nurture and enhance their children's academic achievement. Parents assume that schools in highly ranked systems are committed to ensuring that each child fulfills his or her potential, and they view the curriculum and school reputation as indicators of this commitment.

So, upon realizing that all is not perfect in the Promised Land, parents and students may experience culture shock when they are not welcomed with open arms. In fact, Black families are confronted by obstacles at nearly every turn. Given that these families have moved to the suburbs, often at great expense, to ensure that their children receive a quality education, we can imagine the self-doubt, confusion, disappointment, and frustration these families experience when faced with ongoing intolerance and injustice.

As a school counselor, I have been proud to see African American parents fight for their children with great courage and determination. These parents have no problem suggesting enhancements to the curriculum or starting culturally diverse after school activities. They volunteer in the classroom and participate in the PTA/PTO. In addition to their school involvement, these parents support their children at home by providing cultural enrichment activities. These parents have refused to allow their minority status to stop them from equipping their children for success.

So why, if parents are doing all they can to ensure their children's academic success, are these African American children who attend the best schools money can buy lagging behind their peers? Unfortunately, African American enrollment in suburban schools often has a negative effect on overall student performance—in grades, participation in advanced placement courses, and self-confidence, according to A. Hue. This negative influence may be the result of continuing social, economic, and educational handicaps imposed on African American students by the dominant society.

In an article in *National Review*, A. Hue says it is a myth that students of color "will perform as well as their White peers in good suburban schools and the reality is that the racial gap exists even in the best suburbs." He goes on to say that "some affluent suburbs did no better than nearby urban areas, and even at the best suburban schools, Blacks on average lagged behind their White classmates."

African American students in predominately White suburban schools experience the same achievement gap that is commonly associated with urban schools. The issue of academic achievement is a pervasive problem even when poverty is not a factor. Clearly African American students in suburban schools require as much attention, care, and consideration as African American students in urban schools.

Our job as parents and educators is to begin to understand the causes of this crisis and implement solutions to level the playing field and empower students to excel in the classroom and the school social scene.

Cultural Capital of African American Students

African American students come from a proud people and a rich culture. One could say that their cultural wealth, or cultural capital, is high and this is their strength.

But cultural capital also refers to the connections, resources, knowledge, and experience one has that can be used to succeed in life. For African Americans, this certainly includes their heritage and pride.

Along with their innate talents and abilities, students bring their cultural capital to the classroom. In an African American school, there would be mutual understanding, a shared culture, among students. When you're in the minority, however, you're greeted with suspicion, silence, and even ridicule. Here is where African American parents must resist passivity. Their children's racial identity depends on it.

A sense of belonging to the community is an essential ingredient in a child's self-worth. Being in the minority can create a sense of isolation, separateness, and the awkwardness that comes with being different. As we all know, *no* child wants to be different. But our children's skin colors, facial features, manner of speaking, even their names, set them apart. We must diligently help our children by reinforcing the beauty of their cultural uniqueness.

At this point I must address the issue of parenting styles, which I see as a cultural issue. In predominately White suburbs, this is a controversial issue among Blacks who tend to see White parents as too permissive. Time and again Black parents tell me how White parents allow their children to "talk to them any kind of way." Respect for adults is a tremendous issue with Black parents.

We recall how we had to treat our own parents. There was no room for error with parents who believed in capital punishment. How many of us heard, "I brought you into this world, and I'll take you out." Today, Black parents are tough with their children, but perhaps not as tough as "back in the day."

In the city, Black parents must deal with survival issues every day, and that reality is reflected in their general approach to parenting. There you'll find even young children taking public transportation by themselves. They go grocery shopping, and they take care of younger siblings. After school they come home, cook, clean, and perform many other duties. They must learn how to budget, and some must find jobs to help support the family. Try doing homework under these conditions! For many families, homework is not a priority. In addition, adult supervision may be minimal, which is why there are so many after school programs in schools, churches, field houses, and recreation centers.

Life is not perfect in the suburbs, but our children are bussed to school, or the so-called "soccer mom" drives the children to school in the family SUV. Schools are clean, well staffed, well organized, and high tech. Parents and teachers are considered partners in educating children. In many homes, one parent is financially able to stay at home (or telecommutes). There are many business owners in the suburbs, so there may even be two parents at home at different times during the day. Children may have certain chores, but their main job is school, and that means homework is the primary evening activity.

Now my descriptions of African American family life may find disagreement among my readers, but I'm trying to show how the realities of life shape parenting styles and the decisions we make. Children in the inner city must learn from an early age how to stay safe, so there is a certain toughness to parenting there. These children grow up fast, and in that sense they can be highly "street smart." On the other hand, children in the suburbs are more sheltered from the harshness of life. Since theoretically basic needs are being met in the suburbs, the residents there have a bit more freedom to focus on other things. In fact, the typical suburban community is "child centered," and many local activities focus on entertaining and educating children.

Tracking and Intra-School Segregation

School tracking practices produce racially separate programs. As a result, African American students suffer from limited educational opportunities. In a study conducted by Oakes, it was concluded that lower-track placement worked to the disadvantage of African American students: "Whether these students began with relatively high or relatively low achievement, those who were placed in lower-level courses showed lesser gains over time than similarly situated students placed in higher-level courses." The results of this study indicated three specific disadvantages facing African American students: "(1) unjustifiable disproportionate and segregative assignments to lower-track classes and exclusion from accelerated classes; (2) inferior opportunities to learn; and (3) lower achievement."

The criteria used to make referrals and placement decisions make segregation within schools a cultural norm. The current state of intra-school segregation favors White students and hinders African Americans and Latinos. This is particularly true when it comes to tracking and sorting students based on ability.

Tatum interviewed 18 upper middle-income African American college students about their adolescent years, specifically their school experiences. These students grew up in suburban, predominately White areas. Their families had access to educational and economic resources that helped prepare them for college and leadership in American society. Their parents' expectations, not the encouragement of teachers, motivated them to excel.

Grossman and Ancess studied the achievement gap between students of color and their White counterparts in 11 suburban school districts in New York City, Newark, New Jersey, and Philadelphia. These districts investigated remedies to narrow the achievement gap. Students attended a weekly two-hour study group that focused on improving math problem solving and study skills. The lead teacher encouraged the students to view this activity as enrichment and not remediation.

Interestingly the students reported they were not encouraged to excel and take advanced courses, nor were they provided with the necessary skills to succeed in a higher-level math class.

Intra-school segregation occurs when African American students are removed from the general population and placed in remedial programs. In his study of intra-school segregation, J. Oakes argues that Black students' lower scores on standard assessments justify referrals to remedial or special education classes. Oakes says,

> "Despite its widespread legitimacy, there is no question that tracking, the assessment practices that support it and the differences in educational opportunity that result from it limit many students' schooling and opportunities and life chances."

Oakes says that in underserved African American schools, intra-school segregation is characterized by the overrepresentation of African American students in special education programs. In suburban schools, intra-school segregation is characterized by the exclusion of African American students from advanced placement courses. Complicating intra-school segregation is race. Parents can never be sure how their children are being judged. If their children are not recommended for an advanced placement class, parents usually assume that discrimination is the culprit.

Advanced Placement

Studies have found that race affects the academic track in which students are assigned. African and Hispanic Americans are over represented in the lower tracks while European and Asian Americans are over represented in the higher tracks.

Students of color tend to be excluded from gifted classes in primary school and from honors and advanced placement courses in junior high and high school. Intra-school segregation negatively impacts the representation of African American students in these programs. Technically, test scores are used to determine whether students will be accepted into advanced programs, but in reality it is the subjectivity of a teacher or counselor's recommendation that keeps so many of our students locked out.

If Black students are not equipped with the necessary skills to achieve academic success, then what measures are taken to ensure equal opportunity for all students? I am not suggesting that Black students receive privileged consideration. I believe that *all* students who desire the challenge of advanced learning should receive special preparation (with the parents' blessings, of course).

Tracking has a long-term impact on not just placement in certain academic programs but choice of college major and career. Students of color are often encouraged to pursue vocational training. Even if they are college bound, they may be unprepared for the rigors of science or technology majors.

Teacher Expectations

From a systemic perspective, the difference between urban and suburban schools is the level of expectations teachers and administrators have of students. Generally, suburban schools demand a lot from their students. The academic programs are accelerated and challenging beyond that of urban schools. Parents who have moved from the suburbs back to the city often complain about the fact that the schools seem to lag at least a grade or two behind suburban schools. Why?

Maybe the answer lies in the expectations teachers, schools, and districts have of their students. Much has been written about the deficit thinking that permeates urban school districts. The expectation of student achievement is so low that everything from curriculum design to classroom management is negatively impacted. In suburban schools, although the programs are accelerated (compared to urban schools), Black students still suffer from the low expectations of their teachers.

Low teacher expectations do not serve our students. African American students are just as capable of high achievement as their White counterparts. They should enjoy the same opportunities to experience challenging academic programs as any other students. Bottom line, when teacher expectations are high, learning flourishes in the classroom.

Teacher expectations also extend to perceptions of parents. When parents are involved, teachers become more accountable. When parents hold their children accountable for homework and classroom behavior; the teachers' expectations of student performance rise. If teachers feel confident their work in the classroom is being supported at home, teachers' expectations of students will be reflected in the curriculum design, the pace and passion of teaching, and in classroom management. This is why it is so important for parents and teachers to work together.

Teachers must avoid measuring African American students against White students. According to Kunjufu and other researchers, the learning styles of African American students tend to differ from those of White students. Thus it is unfair to judge African American students by White learning style standards. A good teacher delivers material in a multiplicity of ways (visually, verbally, kinesthetically, etc.) so that all students can benefit from the lessons.

Chapter 1: Education and the Black Family

A teacher's expectations may operate at a subconscious level, but for the sake of our children, this issue must rise to conscious awareness. Teachers with the best of intentions and a strong belief in their students' ability to succeed can make high academic achievement a national standard rather than the province of a selected fortunate few.

Teacher Efficacy

Teacher efficacy is the teacher's confidence in her ability to promote student learning. Bandera defines teacher efficacy as the belief in one's ability to achieve success in a given situation. Carter adds that teacher efficacy relates to the extent in which a teacher believes he or she can teach children and make a difference in their lives.

Low teacher efficacy is one of the characteristics associated with the low achievement of African American students. Do White teachers believe they can truly help African American students perform at a high academic level? Do they believe their African American students are teachable? Do these teachers really believe they can positively impact low achieving students? Do White middle-class values prejudice a teacher's belief in the ability of African American students to learn?

Carter contends that efficacy and expectations are associated with student achievement, specifically among students in diverse classrooms. Carter further adds that many new teachers possess a low sense of efficacy when teaching students from diverse backgrounds. These teachers believe their efforts are tied to students' situational factors. In other words, success or failure in the classroom is tied to poverty and race. This is deficit thinking, and it creates a climate of victimization among students.

On the other hand, teachers with a high sense of efficacy believe their hard work will bring success. Teachers who maintain a high sense of efficacy believe that effort instead of situational factors determine positive outcomes in the classroom.

Chapter 2: Meet the Mothers

In this study I allow the actual words of the mothers to explain events, perceptions, and emotions. In normal everyday life, it may be tempting to perceive these stories as anomalous mishaps, unfortunate situations, a mother venting or misunderstanding the true nature of events. Presented together as I have in this work, however, a big picture emerges of what life is really like for African American families in predominately White suburbs.

As I conducted the individual interviews, I was often surprised at how even the language of the mothers was the same. For example, when talking about their children's interactions with White teachers, they made statements such as, "It's a continuous struggle," "There's always a battle," and "It's been hell." To the best of my ability, I have taken great care to maintain and allow the mothers' words to reveal their great passion and emotion. These endearing, passionate narratives reveal tremendous concern for their children's psychological and educational welfare.

Three main questions guided my research and interviews with the mothers. The questions were:
1. How do you feel about your children's interactions with their White teachers?
2. What difficulties have your children experienced in the classroom?
3. How have your perceptions impacted your role as a parent?

The individual interviews allowed the mothers to share their experiences, while the group sessions allowed for further investigation.

Save Our Children
The Struggle between Black Families and Schools

In this section we will finally meet the mothers who generously gave of their time, experiences, and insights to participate in the study. Their resumes demonstrate an impressive array of professional expertise.

Pseudonyms replaced the participants' names to ensure anonymous and confidential responses.

Lytia. A native of Louisiana, Lytia has lived in the suburban area for approximately five years. She is single with one son in junior high. She is quiet in nature but profound in action. She is a certified school nurse and is currently working on her master's degree. Her future plans include opening a community center for the elderly that will meet their medical, spiritual, and social needs.

Nia. Nia is a native of Michigan and has lived in the suburban area for five years. She is married to a successful executive of a major corporation. They have been married for 20 years and have three children, two of whom are in junior high school. Nia has a bachelor's degree in social work and is currently a full-time wife and mother. Previously Nia worked as a consultant for a school district that had lawsuits filed against it for mistreating students of color. She believes that being a mother is a calling. She contributed more than 200 volunteer hours to her children's school the previous year. She wants to help create systemic change in the school district.

Sheila. Sheila is from Houston and has lived in the suburban area for three years. She and her husband were raised in a rural area and are both products of integration. Sheila's husband is a retired engineer from a major oil company who spends his free time playing golf. They have one adopted daughter whom they have raised since infancy. She is currently 13 years old and in the seventh grade. Sheila is a retired corporate attorney of a major oil company. The move from an affluent African American neighborhood in a large city to a predominately White suburban community was a major change for them. Sheila views herself as a mover and shaker, someone who makes things happen.

Barbara. Barbara is a native of New Mexico. Her husband is a high-ranking officer in the military whose job has caused them to relocate frequently. They have two sons, one in junior high and one a junior in college. Barbara earned an associate's degree from a community college in New Mexico. She has a "laid back" personality and believes in persistently chiseling away at problems. Barbara is a frequent volunteer at her son's school.

Condi. Condi has been a resident in her particular suburban community for 17 years. Her husband is a lawyer and a professional writer who has self-published his first novel. They have two children, a son in junior high and a daughter in high school. Condi has a master's degree in social studies and is currently working on a Ph.D. Her research involves integrating social studies and technology in the curriculum. Condi is a stay-at-home mother who volunteers in her children's schools as well as in the community. She serves on several boards, including a campus-based decision-making committee. Condi is an interesting participant because she has been privy to the district's policies. She understands her rights as a parent, and she helps other mothers understand their rights as well. Condi is considering running for a school board position in the next election.

Theresa. Theresa is a native of Louisiana and has lived in the suburban area for 17 years. She and her husband, a district manager in the food industry, were high school sweethearts. They have two children, a son and daughter, both in junior high. Although she has been a stay-home mom, she recently returned to work as a teacher's aide and is completing her degree to become a special education teacher. Theresa views herself as proactive and outspoken about her culture and her children's school experiences. She is an activist for the rights of African Americans.

The narratives of these six mothers are filled with various emotions, including frustration, anger, disgust, sadness, and even sorrow. This study allowed them to release some of those pent-up emotions. As Nia said,

> "I want to say thank you for doing this, because I know this is a risk for you. I hope you understand that some will love you for doing this and some will hate you. I have a strong belief that you know my children will be overcomers. Some went before us to steal away and read a book or a Bible by candlelight even though it would mean they would receive a lashing or death if they were caught. So we take education very seriously. Education gives us the opportunity to live in these neighborhoods and receive a quality education. Thank you for sharing my story."

Sheila said,

> "It is not enough for you to gather this material and move on to the next level and think, 'Gee, that's a recognizable event.' You are charged with doing something about the situation. You can do that respectfully. You can do that within the law, but do something about it! Let our

voices be heard. Don't let it be reduced to some pages in a book."

Condi added, "This study is going to be the tool to usher in a change. Maybe our Caucasian counterparts will see we are not making this up, and we are not going to change the world, but if we could, change a handful."

I was moved as I listened to these mothers speak their hearts. They were committed to improving the educational opportunities for African American students, not an easy thing to do. So I accepted the challenge that tugged at my heart. The challenge became a calling. I heard the mothers say, "We Want You!" in the same way America says, "Uncle Sam Wants You!" This motto guided my research, analysis, and finally, the writing of this book.

Chapter 3: The Promised Land and Great Expectations

Imagine the Jones family. This mythical African American family lives in a large urban city. With a toddler about to enter kindergarten next year and a new baby on the way, Mr. and Mrs. Jones have been talking a lot about their children's education. They must decide between enrolling them in the neighborhood school which, according to their investigation, is in crisis, or send them to a private school.

They look into some of the private schools in the area. Although they are all quite reputable, they are just too expensive. The tuition at some private schools is as much as college. That would be 13 years (including kindergarten) of paying college level tuition, not to mention saving for actual college.

As they discuss this important issue they realize there is a third option that they had never seriously considered before: they could move to a community where the public schools are like private schools. It would be like sending their children to private school for "free."

So Mr. and Mrs. Jones make the financially challenging but exciting decision to risk everything and move to a suburban community for the sole purpose of getting the children into a great school system. They do their homework. They compare school districts and even make a couple of field trips to see for themselves. Yes the communities could use more racial diversity, but that was a small price to pay for the benefits.

They narrow their investigation to a popular suburb that has two nationally and internationally ranked school districts. The homes are expensive, but they figure they'll be able to find a small one for a reasonable price. Because so many families are making the same decision, purchasing a home in the area is an excellent investment. They checked, and home values have risen steadily over the years. Besides, they'll save in other ways. Gas is not as expensive as in the city, nor are insurance rates. Even food is cheaper.

Mr. and Mrs. Jones drive through the subdivisions (suburban neighborhoods). They love the cleanliness and peacefulness of the streets, and the homes, even the small ones, are really nice. The yards are well kept, and they are heartened to see children playing outside, seemingly without a care in the world.

They go to a park to let their children play. The White parents, who seem friendly enough, have only good things to say about the schools. Textbooks are relevant and up-to-date. The curriculum is challenging, creatively delivered, and engaging. There is a spirit of friendly competition among the students, and the focus is on college preparation. Education is highly valued, and there is a high degree of parental participation. Among the teachers, there is an extraordinarily high percentage with master's and Ph.D. degrees. The top colleges and universities regularly scout for students here.

Unlike many districts throughout the country, the arts are still going strong in this suburb. All schools, even elementary schools, have choir and orchestra programs. Gym is offered *every* day, unlike their current neighborhood school in the city. In fact, fun gym activities often include rock climbing, bowling, horseback riding, and ice skating. High school sports are big in the town.

What finally sells Mr. and Mrs. Jones, however, is the fact that suburban schools are accelerated above and beyond urban schools by *one to three grade levels*. They could hardly believe it! It was as if *all* the schools in the suburb were gifted and talented. No matter where a child was academically and intellectually, he or she had access to the best teachers, the best curriculum, and the safest schools money could buy.

Mr. and Mrs. Jones had mixed feelings about this. On one hand, they didn't disparage White parents for being able to send their children to outstanding neighborhood schools. Every child deserved the best education. But why couldn't all children attend amazing schools? Why wasn't that a minimum standard in America? Whatever happened to equal access to educational opportunities? African Americans fought and died for this right. As homeowners in the city, Mr. and Mrs. Jones pay property taxes to fund education just as suburban homeowners do. Why aren't all city schools accelerated like suburban schools? Why isn't there a level playing field?

In the city, an accelerated education is not a right for all children like in the suburbs. Only a tiny minority of students who pass the gifted and talented test is allowed into so-called "magnet" schools. The test is given only once a year, and it is not widely publicized. In the city, if a student does not pass the gifted and talented test by even a couple of points, he or she must go the neighborhood school or an expensive private school. Few neighborhood schools offer programs that meet the needs of gifted students or students who have tremendous potential. There are charter schools, but the waiting lists are long for the better ones. Getting in is often a political exercise, and the Joneses don't know anyone in the system who could help them.

To add insult to injury, gifted and talented programs in city schools are on par academically with *regular* programs in the suburbs.

Save Our Children
The Struggle between Black Families and Schools

Mr. and Mrs. Jones get angry. They wouldn't have to move away from family, friends, and all they hold dear if *all* the schools in the city were accelerated like in the suburbs. It wasn't fair. Surely the educational powers in the city knew about this amazing suburban model?

The bottom line is Mr. and Mrs. Jones want the best educational opportunity for their children. So they decide to do whatever it takes to move to the Promised Land, the suburbs. They hate the inequities in the system, but they must do the right thing for their children, and they strongly believe that moving is the right thing to do. Their expectations are high, and despite their concerns about diversity, they're excited. Little do they know, but educating an African American child in the suburbs can be just as challenging (or more) as in the city.

* * *

The stories may differ in narrative, but the plot is often the same for African American families who move to the suburbs in search of educational opportunities for their children. As the mothers in this study discovered, all is not well in the suburbs. Often these schools do not live up to their promise, especially when it comes to educating African American children.

The mothers all said that despite taking purposeful steps to prepare their children for success, academic achievement was often elusive which, after having such high expectations, was demoralizing. Thus the mothers all felt that they needed to take special care so that their children would not sink into frustration and despair.

1. The mothers continue to maintain high expectations of their children even while working to improve teacher interactions.
2. They constantly work on building their children's self-esteem. Children are encouraged verbally, and they participate in various social activities outside of school.

Theresa sounded sad and exhausted during one particular interview as she talked about her children's schools. She had learned a lot about the schools through her volunteering experiences. After a conversation with one of her daughter's teachers, Theresa began to believe the teacher felt that African American parents and students wanted something they did not deserve. She felt the teacher wished her child would go away because she was an intrusion upon her middle-income White comfort zone. Theresa said, "We are here. We are not going anywhere, and they need to realize that we are not asking for handouts. We do not want special treatment. We just want what any parent wants. We want what's best for our kids."

High Expectations of School

The school district in the study was, according to the mothers, the best in the state. This assessment was based on test scores, reports from the state's education agency, reports on the Internet, educational publications, and word-of-mouth.

Theresa and her husband decided to move into the school district because they believed it would prepare their children for higher education. Theresa's parents were already living in the area and often talked about how great the district was.

"That's why I am here, because I heard this was a good school district. The kids scored well on tests—they were able to pass the SAT. They were preparing these kids for a higher education, and that is what we want for our kids. I want my kids to go to college; they want to go to college. I just want them to be prepared."

Nia once worked as a consultant in a school district in the Northwest. She helped the district develop strategies to decrease the mistreatment of students of color. When her husband was offered a job transfer, they chose the school district out of several based on the reputation of the schools alone.

"I came to the district because of research via the Internet. I was looking for schools that would be good for all children and that was my expectation. I feel that I am not a parent that is not uninformed about how schools work. So when I saw the statistics and I saw the things that were necessary, I felt like this district had what I was looking for. I wanted my children in the public arena because I didn't want them secluded in a private setting where they didn't get a taste of the variety of what could be offered to them through a public school experience."

Sheila and her husband were in the process of deciding about retirement options when they began researching school districts. They wanted to relocate to a "good" neighborhood to provide their daughter with the best possible educational opportunities.

> "I decided there are some good public schools around here, so my husband and I did our research, did our homework, and that is how we came to be in this district. We thought, since the district was thriving—there was so much new construction, and there were so many professional transferees in my neighborhood— this district would be a good choice. So I went online. In addition, I talked quite frequently to the state's education agency for information. They sent me booklets on where the best school districts were. So based on that information, we came here."

Lytia moved to the suburbs from an underserved community in Louisiana where the schools lacked up-to-date textbooks and adequate supplies. She desired a better environment for her son. She did not want the lack of books and resources to prevent him from receiving a quality education. Friends she knew in the suburban school district suggested she move there.

> "I am from Louisiana and the schools there cannot be compared to the schools here. There are some areas in Louisiana without adequate supplies for the students. Some students have to go without textbooks if their parents cannot afford them. I heard about this school district

from friends. I then came here to visit and decided that I would like for my son to have the opportunity to receive an education in this district. Publications I read gave this district rave reviews. My son's school was also featured in a national publication for being one of the top ten schools with the highest test scores in the state. I was extremely impressed. We moved and here we are."

High Expectations of Students

When it comes to their children's academic performance and success in life, the parents have high expectations. They constantly communicate their expectations to their children and teachers. If necessary, they provide tutoring to help them meet the demands of the classroom. As Nia said,

> "I always talk to my children in terms of when you own a company or when you go to Med school—*when*, not if. Or even if they work for someone, I want them to understand that God has given them gifts and they are to be used greatly. So, our pictures are big, they are not small."

The parents have high expectations for their children's grades. They expect them to work to their potential, and they encourage them to set high goals for themselves. Theresa contacted one of her daughter's advanced placement teachers after her daughter brought home a C on an assignment. Apparently the teacher felt that Theresa was overreacting.

Her daughter received the C for a reason, and Theresa wanted to find out just what that reason was. She wanted to help her daughter modify her behavior so that she would receive a higher grade in the future. Theresa believed her daughter was fully capable of earning a higher grade.

> "I spoke with the teacher about the C, and the teacher acted like, 'What's the big deal?' I said, 'Because my daughter is not a C student— that's the big deal.' It seemed like that was good enough for the teacher, but it was not good enough for me, especially when I know my daughter's capabilities. She is capable of making an A and that is what we shoot for, A's not C's."

The beliefs held by the mothers have been proven by their children's accomplishments. The children have received many awards and honors, some based on academic achievement, others for involvement in extracurricular activities. All children have participated in the Duke University Talent Identification Program (TIP), which gives them the opportunity to take the SAT or ACT as seventh graders. Collectively they have won science fairs, received perfect scores on state-mandated assessments, and have had their creative writings published.

The children have been exposed to a wide range of experiences, from educational family vacations to business trips. The children have participated in organized social activities including sports, dance, and theater. Some have won awards for band and stage productions. The parents read to their children, make frequent trips to public libraries, and visit museums, nationally and internationally.

The mothers believe that exposing their children to service learning experiences is important. They have served others in shelters and gone on mission trips to work with less fortunate populations.

Self-Esteem and Cultural Capital

Vincent (2001) states that middle-income parents have enough cultural capital (connections, resources, knowledge, and experience) to aggressively pursue improvements in their children's school experience. The cultural capital of the family gives a child inner resiliency and self-esteem. Parents are empowered by their cultural capital to make positive changes in the classroom, school, and school district.

The mothers agree with Anderson (1988), a scholar who viewed education as a means to liberation and freedom as well as a mechanism against oppression. They are consciously aware that they and their families stand on the gains made by African Americans throughout history, e.g., the landmark case of *Brown v. the Board of Education.* This proud heritage is a significant cultural asset.

Time and again, the mothers have drawn on their vast reserves of cultural capital, especially when they noticed how their children's "spirits were broken" and "self-esteem was damaged" because of their classroom experiences. The mothers remembered how vibrant and lively their children had been prior to entering these schools. They spoke about their children being fun-loving and excited to learn, and they also remembered specific moments when they realized their children were drained, unhappy, and unenthusiastic about their learning experiences.

"I feel like you build that self-esteem not by telling them but by showing them. So, we would do outside activities where she had success. And in every area she would thrive," said Nia about her daughter. For example, Nia's daughter has received national awards in Tae Kwon Do. She also received national recognition in a university program. Unfortunately, her successes were not recognized at her school.

"You just hope that you can gather enough self-esteem and enough joyous experiences to counteract what they do to your children," said Sheila.

There was sadness in the voices of these mothers as they told their stories. However, a testimony to their inner resiliency and their parents' determination, the students have still scored well on standardized exams, and they remain in their advanced placement courses.

Chapter 4: The Advanced Placement Struggle

Regarding the ongoing battle to prepare, enroll, and keep their children in advanced placement classes, the perceptions of the mothers can be categorized according to the following four themes:
1. Teachers' lack of cultural appreciation.
2. Low expectations held by teachers (students constantly had to prove their ability).
3. Lack of communication from teacher to parent.
4. Teachers' lack of appreciation for the lengths to which African American families prepared for their children's success.

During the first days and weeks in their new schools and when problems first began to arise, the mothers gave the teachers the benefit of the doubt. It was possible that the fault lay with their children. Eventually, however, they began to realize that these experiences were not typical. They began to believe their children were being treated unfairly.

It was important for the mothers to know what questions to ask during registration and conferences regarding placement into preparatory and advanced placement courses. The mothers left school conferences reconsidering the decision to enroll their children in the school. Needless to say, their first impressions of the school and district were not positive. They felt that the White teachers were not motivated to teach their African American students and that *race* was the culprit. They felt that White educators were biased against their children because of the stereotypes that plague African Americans to this day.

It was at the beginning of seventh grade when Sheila realized that the teacher did not want her daughter in the classroom. She said the teacher excluded her daughter from classroom discussions.

> "My daughter is being treated like a second-class citizen. I don't feel like the teachers get it. I think because of their background and some of their expectations of dealing with people of color that when they encountered someone like us they take it personally when I am only trying to get the best for my child. I know there is prejudice, but it should not enter that classroom door. They should leave that at the front door and pick it up when they go home."

Lytia said,

> "Because the teachers' upbringing was totally different from ours—they lived through segregation—things were different for them and so they were accustomed to living a certain way."

One of the criteria for participants in this study was to have a child who qualified for pre-advanced placement courses (the junior high version of the advanced placement in high school), but was asked or recommended to exit the class. Advanced placement courses have been a focal point of this research because the students who participate in these courses are bright students and have the ability to excel academically.

The preparatory classes ready students for higher education by increasing grade point averages and improving class rank. Students are taught to think critically and analytically in advanced placement courses. The mothers support the curriculum because they mirror the high expectations they have for their children.

Sheila's desire to place her child in an advanced placement course was frustrated by an important gatekeeper: the school guidance counselor. Sheila recalled how the counselor tried to convince her that her daughter did not belong in advanced placement. Sheila knew her child was able to handle the course, but the counselor was not willing to listen to Sheila's concerns. At this point, Sheila was grateful for her corporate background which she says taught her how to deal with White people who were not willing to give African Americans the benefit of the doubt. Sheila remembered looking at her daughter and seeing a puzzled look on her face.

> "Had I not been exposed to a corporate environment and had I not known what questions to ask, I think I would have walked out of registration as bewildered as my child. I guess my experience with this school was with registration and there was not any support. After I told them I am from a different school district, it did not matter. It was at that point I could see that it was going to be sink or swim."

The registration experience was impersonal. Apparently a script was used and students were expected to fit a certain mold. If they did not fit that mold, there was no support. Barbara, Condi, and Nia said that fitting the mold also was expected in other areas of the classroom experience as well.

At Sheila's conference, the teacher presented a paper her daughter had written. Based on that assignment, it was recommended that her daughter exit the course. Sheila did not agree, and the teacher became angry.

> "The teacher threw up her hands very demonstrative and said, 'I don't understand her—her thoughts seemed jumbled and look at this paper.' She read it out loud and it sounded pretty good to me. I guess that was my first experience with her. Okay, so she is different. You should embrace difference. Not everybody is going to write the same, talk the same, or act the same. They said she was talkative. I said that is an attribute of a Black child. They did not want her talking a lot so that let me know right then that what she was supposed to do was sit in one of those chairs, preferably in the back, and not make any trouble. It was horrible from then on."

Sheila left the conference feeling that this teacher did not accept her daughter because she was different. There was no acceptance of cultural differences.

Theresa faced a similar situation when her daughter was asked to exit an advanced placement course. Theresa's daughter was doing quite well in the beginning and then she began to struggle. Theresa felt it was a shame that the teacher could think of nothing else but to remove her daughter from an important class. Nor would she offer an alternative plan to bring her up to speed. That was unacceptable.

> "My daughter started out doing well in the advanced placement courses. She was in seventh grade, and I believe the pressure from being a Black young lady in a predominantly White school added more pressure and her grades started to fall. The teacher and counselor wanted to take her out of the classes and I said, 'No.' I told them I would provide tutoring opportunities. I suggested we meet to discuss my child because I know my child's capabilities and we need to try to work together to keep her in these courses."

Barbara said her son's teachers wanted him out of advanced placement courses before they realized his capability. Moreover, they did not want any discussion with her.

> "He was in all pre-advanced placement courses, and it started right away. The teachers said he was misplaced. Because of the teachers' continual prompting, I took him out of advanced math, but he remained in the other advanced placement classes and it has been a struggle."

Condi's daughter was in an advanced reading course, and she was having some difficulty understanding a novel that had been assigned. In a meeting with the teacher, it was recommended that her daughter exit the course. Condi was frustrated. She said,

> "The novel had difficult language and was difficult for kids to relate to. The teacher said if it was too difficult for her then perhaps we needed to consider removing her since she was struggling. She suggested we move her to an academic class."

Lytia said,

> "I went to the teacher to discuss what was going on. I got the impression that the teacher did not believe that he was able to keep up with the pace of the advanced class because he asked a lot of questions. I also believe the teacher did not believe he belonged in the class because he questioned her assignments. He began to struggle because he did not feel comfortable asking the teacher questions. When his grades began to fall, the teacher asked me to consider moving him to a lower level class."

At Open House, her son's White teachers appeared uncomfortable talking to her. The teacher would not make eye contact with Lytia and didn't seem to accept her questions. Lytia left the school with great concern for her son who had to sit under a teacher who appeared uncomfortable around African Americans.

Nia said,

"I believe these teachers do not want to try
hard because they believe our children should
not be in their advanced placement classes. The
teachers did not want my daughter in any
PreAp courses. I did not understand that
because her grades were good from her
previous school. The teachers said they did not
recommend her for these classes, and I heard
comments, such as whether she had certain
capabilities. I knew many of the students in
those classes because I knew their parents.
Those White kids did not have the capabilities
they were expecting to see in my child. For
the White students the teachers see potential.
For ours they see problems."

It wasn't clear to the mothers how the teachers drew
these conclusions so quickly when it was only the beginning
of the school year. Lytia said that although her son had
excellent state test scores, he asked too many questions during
classroom discussions. The teacher probably assumed he
should have known the material already. Instead of embracing
a difference in the student, the only option was to say that he
was misplaced.
    Sheila said,

"Two weeks into the school year (so that was
the end of August), we were called together,
my husband and I, to meet with my daughter's
team of teachers. We were told that she was

not pre-advanced 'material,' and of course, the first thing we asked was, 'What is the basis of that?' Well, you don't have a basis because you have not had any tests or maybe one. If you look at her standardized test scores, you will see that she qualifies to be in this class."

Sheila said the teacher ignored the test scores and refused to give her daughter the opportunity to be successful in the class.

Simpson (2001) believes that students who meet the criteria for acceptance into advanced courses are more likely to be turned away based on the recommendation of a counselor or teacher. Simpson and these mothers further believe that placement into advanced courses is contingent on ability, past achievement, and socioeconomic status. Race also affects the placement of students. Apparently there is little regard for the fact that the students are high achievers and have highly involved parents who have demonstrated their commitment to provide the best educational opportunities for their children.

The mothers have had to fight many exhausting battles, and they have been left battle fatigued and war scarred by their interactions with teachers and school administrators. These initial battles mentioned in this chapter were only the beginning of what has turned out to be a long, intractable war. Still, the mothers try their best to prevent negativity to taint their children's experiences at school. They are determined to provide a quality educational experience for their children in the suburbs.

Chapter 5: Racism in the Schools

The lack of cultural appreciation among White teachers is associated with the history of desegregation. School desegregation, a noble and important goal of the civil rights movement, has not always served the best interests of African American families. From the time of *Brown v. the Board of Education*, school desegregation has been seen as a means of providing African American students access to White schools, their resources and educational opportunities. Although African Americans were allowed in the classrooms as desegregation became the law of the land, unfortunately, the hearts of White people were slow to change. African American students were not embraced. In fact, White parents took their children out of schools rather than have them sit next to a Black child. Some parents took their children out of the entire system to prevent them from being bussed to predominately Black schools.

The mothers in the study had a lot to say about the cultural climate in their children's schools. They all believed that teachers and administrators lacked an appreciation for cultural diversity. Their bigotry arose time and again in the classroom. In fact, the history curriculum, specifically lessons about slavery and the civil rights movement, were brutal. The lack of cultural sensitivity was horrifying for the students and the mothers. The insensitive manner in which the lessons were taught as well as negative comments made by classmates were unbearable. The African American students were ostracized and made fun of during these highly sensitive lessons, and the teachers failed to seize the opportunity to discuss cultural acceptance. Sheila said,

"They were discussing the slave chapter in our state's history. One of the students read a passage from the book then looked around and pointed at my daughter and said, 'You were a slave and my people owned your people.' And, of course, she was upset by that. That was kind of cruel. Rather than the teacher taking that kid aside and saying, 'Look, we are all in this together,' in other words, *say something*, she said nothing. My daughter came home upset about it. I called the teacher and she finally called me back and said that was hearsay. She was sure little Johnnie [the White student who made the comment] did not say all of that. In other words, 'Whatever you say over there, you are just a troublemaker, and you are asking for special treatment. Just go ahead and get along no matter how you feel.'"

Because the teacher did not embrace cultural appreciation, Sheila's daughter was left to deal with her feelings on her own. Also, the administration failed to hold the teacher accountable for her terrible handling of the situation.

Condi said,

"My daughter came home and told me that her social studies teacher said that slavery was not bad because the slaves were fed and given shelter and that actually freeing them had more of a negative impact than being slaves."

Chapter 5: Racism in the Schools

Condi was extremely angry when her daughter shared this information with her. She could not believe that a teacher could be this insensitive. Condi said she would go to the school to talk to the teacher, but her daughter said she would talk to him because she did not want her mother to come to the school. She allowed her daughter to handle the situation. Condi told her daughter,

> "Go back to school tomorrow and tell him that I said in no uncertain terms there was no positive aspect to slavery. To tell the students in his room otherwise, that's just beyond criminal. That's horrible, and she did tell him."

Other participants shared similar examples of how slavery lessons were delivered and that were just as horrific.

Lytia said she did not see any bulletin boards or any pictures hanging on the walls that would indicate diversity and a climate of cultural acceptance. In fact, her son was called a nigger by a classmate in the locker room. Apparently he was expected to just get over it. His teachers did not have any idea of how cruel and insensitive this experience was. Lytia feared her son's educational experience would suffer in the long run.

> "Throughout the year, I did not see anything that showed me the teachers were culturally sensitive. I did not see any celebrations of diversity. I did not see anything that would make my son feel like his school embraced a system that incorporated culture into his daily experience. However, my son experienced

being called a nigger, and I do not believe the students who called him that were punished because it was their word against my son's. I called the school and talked to the principal and he assured me that he would look into it. Not only did I have to deal with that situation, but a few weeks later I received a call to say that my son was searched in the principal's office because someone reported that he had a knife in his pocket. It was a plastic knife from the school cafeteria."

Lytia became very angry as she shared her story. She paused, then took a deep breath and continued with another experience. The following incident occurred after her son was called the racial slur. She received a phone call at work from her son's school. He had been called into the principal's office after lunch.

"I was at my breaking point when I received a call from the principal's office that said the police were in his office talking to my son. I remember leaving my job and feeling rage. I kept thinking to myself, 'Why do they hate my son so much? He is very social, but he is not a criminal. What is the problem?' I arrived at the school to find my son crying and afraid. I instructed him not to say another word, thinking that he would need an attorney."

Lytia said that although the incident was an accident, the police were called by the parent and they had to do their job. Lytia's son had to appear before a judge. She talked about how traumatic this experience was for her son. She said she moved him to this district from an inner city school in another state because she was trying to avoid situations like this. The school did not embrace her son's culture and was quick to react to a negative experience without consideration of his good character.

Barbara's son was also called a nigger in the locker room by a White student. Barbara's son became angry and wanted to react. The student was disciplined, but Barbara felt the administration and the coaches also should have addressed the issue with her son, but they did not. She believed the administration handled the situation according to the discipline plan without regard to the emotional or cultural impact the incident had on her son.

> "My son was called a nigger in the locker room during his athletics class. The student who called him this name was disciplined, but my son was left to deal with this incident at home. He was angry and wanted to react. He said he realized that he would get into trouble, although he felt justified in fighting the student. My husband handled that situation by spending the evening with our son to shed insight about the racism that exists in the world."

The mothers believed that the teachers should have handled these experiences differently. Had the teachers been more tolerant and understanding of other cultures, they might have handled these situations in ways that would have allowed the children's dignity, pride, and self-esteem to remain in tact. In addition, these events could have served as "teachable moments," in which White students could have learned more about their African American classmates. Instead these children were left with feelings of bewilderment and embarrassment in the midst of a culturally insensitive climate, and the ignorance of the White students remains to this day.

Cooperative learning projects were another source of White hostility against the African American students. Sheila said her child's project partners did not want to work with her in a group project, so the daughter was given menial tasks. Instead of the teacher seizing the opportunity to teach cultural appreciation, her child was removed from the group and given an individual assignment.

> "My daughter [the only African American student in the classroom] wrote some ideas on a piece of paper and a student threw it on the floor because she did not want to use her ideas. Then she told my daughter to pick up the paper and she refused. The teacher then removed my daughter from the group (which I did not agree with) because she says she was not cooperating. So, what I find going on over there is that rather than make trouble for the White counterpart, they just sort of smooth things over or they treat you like it's your fault when something happens. You are not getting along with the rest of the children."

This parent was so angry she had difficulty telling her story. Sheila's daughter received an A on her individual project that was originally designed to be a group effort. She framed the assignment and hung it over her daughter's bed. This assignment represents many things, including a child's

48

struggle against systemic racism in the school district and the lack of cultural appreciation among White teachers and students.

Nia's daughter was the only African American in her class. She participated in a science competition with a team that previously won the award for best in the city. To compete on the team, Nia's daughter had to make up a test she had missed. Unfortunately, after several attempts to make up the test, the teacher failed to allow her to take it. The teacher kept putting her off for different reasons. Then, to make matters worse, she gave Nia's daughter an incomplete for the class. This made the student ineligible to compete, thus disqualifying her and the team from competing in the state championship.

Children should not be penalized for teachers' inability to create an accepting and culturally sensitive environment. The mothers in this study do not believe the teachers have their children's best interests at heart. They believe their children were barely tolerated, and the teachers seemed unwilling to at least try and appreciate their African American culture. Is it possible that this insensitive environment affected the performance of these African American students?

If the teachers had only communicated with the students and parents the situation could have been improved. Communication is a vital building block in relations with parents and students. In fact, the mothers made themselves available to talk to the teachers, but to no avail. Ironically, in an era of advanced communication technologies, never had talking been so difficult. The mothers offered their home, cell, and work phone numbers. They offered their own and their husbands' email addresses. Nia even offered her neighbor's phone number.

Because the teachers refused to communicate with them, report cards were always a big surprise. For example, the student might be passing at the mid-term point but would have a failing grade on the report card. Also, for some strange reason, their grade point averages would often end in nine (e.g., 69, 79, or 89). This made the mothers suspicious. Had an error been made? What could the children have done to improve their grades? The mothers did not know. Simple communication before the end of the term could have answered these questions, but the teachers refused to talk.

"Why does it have to be so difficult?" asked Theresa. "I am just asking for enlightenment. I am not saying give me the answers. Just explain to me what you want."

Lytia said,

> "The teacher emailed me once, and this is after coming to her twice and giving her my email address. I said to her, 'Talk to me about my son. Let me know what's going on with him.' I don't think they made any effort to say, 'You guys feel free to call us. We're here for you.' I mean, even setting up a meeting was a hassle to me. It was never when I can do it. It was always work around the teacher's schedule. I left many invitations for her to call me at work and I also left her my cell phone number. If there was something she thought I needed to know or that we needed to work on at home, give me a call. 'You know we will do it.' Never once received a phone call about when he was doing well or when he was slacking. I never received a phone call at all. You can tell those teachers who do not know how to communicate with anyone other than Caucasians. Or

maybe they know how to communicate, they just do not want to communicate with me and it shows. As far as this teacher communicating with me, our conversations have been far and few in between."

Condi said,

"My daughter took an exam and received a 75 on it. There was no contact from the teacher. There was never any feedback from this particular teacher. I personally felt she could do a lot better, but the teacher accepted that as her score. I was very disappointed by the teacher's lack of interest in my daughter's performance. I decided to email the teacher. I asked her if she could notify me if my daughter's grade began to drop and if she did not turn in assignments."

The mothers pleaded with the teachers to communicate with them. They deserved the same communication White parents received. Nia became so fed up she began to copy the principal whenever she emailed a teacher. Then and only then would she get a response. That led to a meeting with the principal. Although she was finally able to express her frustration, she began to sense that the lack of communication was an accepted practice in the school.

One of the teachers asked the principal, "Why does she have to know what her child's grade is every quarter? Why can't she just let me teach her child?" The principal responded, "Why do you always have to know what your children's grades are?" The response, which could have been made by any of the mothers in the study, was, "Because I have a right. I have a right like every parent in this school. You do it for other parents in this school, but I seem to be the parent that you have a problem with."

Nia said that African American parents who inquire about their children's progress are viewed as troublemakers. If White parents inquire about their children, then they are helpful parents. "They always had a reason or there was something that justified why they didn't have to respond to us," said Nia. These mothers were extremely frustrated with not only the lack of communication but also the seemingly endless struggles their children faced in the classroom. In an article in the *Journal of Educational Policy* entitled "Social Class and Parental Agency," C. Vincent contends that middle-income African American parents have a sense of entitlement because their educational background empowers them to challenge the expert (i.e., the educator). Vincent says "educational awareness" and "interconnectedness" between family and school life can potentially lead to a shared responsibility between teacher and parent, a true partnership.

There has been much discussion regarding the utter breakdown of communication and relationship between African American parents and teachers in the inner city. Parents don't trust teachers, and teachers don't trust parents. What little communication exists is hostile. Arguments sometimes occur in front of students.

My point is that African American children are not being served in the classroom whether in the privileged suburbs or the underserved inner city. Our children come first. Teachers and parents must begin to respectfully and regularly communicate for the sake of the children.

Chapter 6: Stereotypes and Low Expectations

Middle-income African American mothers believe their children have to constantly prove themselves to their teachers. White students are viewed as having potential, but African American students are viewed as having problems. Nia said her children's teachers refused to give them the benefit of the doubt when it came to classroom performance.

> "I think it's a huge burden on a child to tell them that a teacher will never respect you when you walk in the door. You have to work your way up, when other children get the advantage of having to work their way down."

Nia believes these teachers had low expectations for the African American students and high expectations for the White students. White students are given the benefit of the doubt, and African American students are not. During enrollment, Nia had to present her daughter's resume of outstanding academic achievement before the counselor would accept her into the advanced placement courses. Apparently test scores are not enough when it comes to African American students. In the classroom, her daughter had to receive an A on an assignment before the teacher would believe she was capable of handling the class.

> "The teachers come in with low expectations and the students have to work their way up. No matter what their records say, no matter what their ability is, the teachers come in with very low expectations. The teachers expect

behavior problems, they expect low grades, they expect that they won't do as well as the other children, and it takes some hard documented evidence that will prove them otherwise. These students cannot win with teachers who have this type of mentality. If you have a teacher in a classroom who doesn't think you should be there, then they do things to validate that you should not be there."

Nia said her daughter was discouraged when her A papers drew no comments or praise, although her White classmates received encouragement. It was not until her child received honors, awards, and national recognition for scores on national exams that her teacher then accepted that she truly belonged in the advanced classes. This was an example of an African American student having to "work her way up" to belong in these classes.

Condi said that teachers accepted African American students if their parents were well known professional athletes, musicians, etc. Condi called this having "star power." She believes that teachers have negative stereotyped beliefs regarding the abilities of African American students, and in their minds, the neglect is justified. But exceptions are made if the teacher believes she has something to gain from knowing the student.

"Preconceived notions can be broken down if they think there is some star power to it, or something like that. Or maybe they figure you don't smell and that you are a typical middle-class family. I still think it is on a case-by-case basis, and I do not think it is all impacting or changing their view of a race. They are willing to accept those few and willing to say you are different because you are not like 'them' in the city."

Condi and the other participants want the teachers to get to know their children, not the stereotypes about them. Unfortunately, they seem willing to do that only when there is something to gain. When there is nothing to gain, there's no reason to communicate or get to know the children or even bother to have high expectations. In fact, Condi cites the low expectations of her daughter's teacher as the reason for the lack of communication.

Barbara felt that her son's teachers just didn't respect him. During conferences, they had nothing good to say about him. Instead they would note all his mistakes. She did not think the White students were receiving the same treatment.

"He was not respected as a student that was learning on the same wavelength or level as the other advanced placement students. I believe he had to work harder to prove himself worthy of being there in the eyes of the teacher."

Barbara believed the way her son dressed influenced the teacher's low expectations of him. His cultural style of clothing represented who he was as an African American youth, and she thinks this offended the teacher.

"I believe they expected my son to attend this school for his athletic abilities. The teachers all know that he is an exceptional basketball player, but that is not why he is in school. I placed him here to get a good education. He loves dressing like a basketball player, in his jersey and basketball tennis shoes. There is much more to him. He has a brain. But I do not know if the teachers can see beyond that. If he does not participate in class or if his grades are not A's or B's, I believe that is fine with them. He is not pushed to work to his potential. Low expectations."

Nia said,

"I don't see teachers giving our students the same benefit of the doubt. I think they hold our students to a level of perfection and they hold the White students to a level of development. They are always seen as potential, even kids who come in and cuss them out or treat them with disrespect. They're in a development stage. Our kids are sent to the principal because they are in a rebellious discipline stage."

Sheila said, "This is an example of low expectations, thinking the worst of my daughter from the very beginning." Her daughter's teacher accused her of lying about some of her grades. The teacher could not find all of the assignments and instead of asking the student, he assumed she was lying and gave her zeros for the missing assignments. When Sheila discovered why her daughter received the zeros, she contacted the teacher and provided the assignments that were in her daughter's folders. Sheila also met with the teacher to discuss the situation. She believed this was an unfair situation that could have been handled differently.

Picking Battles to Win the War

Sometimes the mothers became weary of fighting this war because it is unrelenting. They have had to learn how to pick their battles. They worried that their advocacy may backfire against their children in the classroom. They feared subtle retaliations from the teachers—retaliations that could not always be proven. Despite this fear, the mothers continued to fight this war because they knew they were fighting for a great prize: equal access to educational opportunities.

The mothers agreed that teachers must avoid measuring African American children against White students. This practice has prevented teachers from improving their own pedagogy around African American learning styles.

Confirmation for the mothers' fears and suspicions came from a surprising source: White parents. Carpooling provided an excellent opportunity to get insider information regarding the attitudes and biases of some White teachers.

Nia once asked her White neighbor to create an email they could both send to their children's teacher. They sent the email that contained the same information requesting feedback to support their children in the advanced placement course. According to Nia, the neighbor received an immediate response that was insightful and helpful. Nia, on the other hand, did not receive a response for about a week, and the response she received was vague.

District, school, and classroom diversity programs must be implemented to meet the needs of all students. It's possible that White teachers are unaware of the prejudices they bring into the classroom and conferences with parents. Their low expectations of African American students may be on a subconscious level. Teacher efficacy, the belief in one's own ability to be effective in the classroom and specifically in this case, with African American students, may be low. Subconscious prejudices against our children may be the cause of low teacher efficacy.

In *Education and Culture,* G. D. Spindler reports that teachers with the best intentions can have both a negative and positive impact on students. They can encourage positive goals in students, but they can also guide students away from trying their best because of their own low expectations.

The bottom line, say the mothers, is that White teachers are often not comfortable teaching African American students. These teachers are not exposed enough to our culture. Their desire to quickly exit African American students out of advanced placement courses and their unwillingness to listen to the mothers suggest a strong resistance to change—change in pedagogy and perhaps, change in their overall life philosophies and beliefs.

Teacher efficacy and teacher expectations have long been associated with student achievement. It is unfortunate that this research has not been transmitted to the many White teachers and administrators who need to change their views. As the mothers say, "Our families are here to stay!"

Many beginning teachers possess a low efficacy when teaching students from diverse backgrounds. The efforts of these teachers will have limited success because they believe situational factors in a student's family life and culture determine success or failure in the classroom. These teachers believe that a middle-income background enhances success in the classroom. If the students are from an impoverished background, then failure is the expectation.

On the other hand, teachers with a high efficacy, a strong belief in their ability to teach African American students, believe their hard work and cultural sensitivity and acceptance will bring success. Those teachers who refuse to make the effort will fail. Knowing this and more, the mothers continue to attempt to work and communicate with their children's teachers.

Chapter 7: Parenting At Its Best

Excellent parenting in the midst of entrenched institutional racism will help ensure that no matter what, children can succeed in school and in life. As I talked to the mothers about the nuts and bolts of parenting in a hostile school situation, three best practice themes emerged: advocacy, visibility, and proactive parenting. These best practices are imperative to the continuing success of their children, and they equip the mothers with the energy needed to fight. The mothers realized they would have to do some things differently in order to help their children survive and thrive.

Advocacy. The mothers realized that they must be advocates for their children. This is an important role and one that seemed to be lacking within the school. The mothers felt that the school system was holding their children responsible for their own learning and refused to provide needed support. The mothers wanted to ensure that the school was held accountable, so they assumed the role of advocate.

Sheila wanted to help her child improve her grades, so she asked the teacher for a syllabus to support the classroom work at home. The teacher said she did not plan any more than a week in advance and was unwilling to give Sheila this information. Sheila told the teacher,

> "That's not my fault. If there is information over there, I am entitled to it, and I am not going to let you talk to me any kind of way. We are not trying to make it seem like you are not doing your job, but we will have the information one way or the other. I will parallel

teach, and I will make sure that my child has an enriched learning environment."

Sheila wanted the resources to support the teacher in the classroom, and it became a problem. However, this parent was not taking no for an answer because she believed having a syllabus was in her child's best interest.

> "When they look at my daughter, they see a little White kid's seat because I have been told that if she is not going to concentrate or do this or do that, there are plenty of others who will take her seat. In other words, that's a White seat. And what I tell them is no-no-no, that's my child's seat. You may consider her a second-class citizen because she is African American, but she is not. She is going to stay right in this class, and the only way you are going to get her out is that I determine whether or not she absolutely cannot do the work."

Sheila realized that she had a say in her child's education, and she felt the need to speak out about the teachers' lack of desire to work with her child.

Visibility. Visibility came to mean more to these mothers than it once did. These mothers actively volunteered in their children's schools. They worked in various areas, including the school store, library, and main office. Nia logged in more than 200 volunteer hours during one school year. The mothers also served on various decision-making committees in the school and the district. Nia said,

"They relate differently to you if you're there than if you are not there. I'll tell you my experience of that. I would be sitting at the welcome desk and the teacher would be coming around the corner and see me and talk to an African American child one way and another way when they did not see me. Then they would fix it and say, 'You know, I was just joking around.'"

Theresa said,

"I have seen where a White mom was volunteering and the teacher went to get her and explain to her what her child was doing instead of sending that student to the office. It just makes you feel like your child is under a microscope all of the time."

Theresa knew her child would never have been given such a pass. Her visibility as a volunteer in the school opened her eyes to the kinds of things that were taking place.

Barbara said,

"If you are visible, they are not going to mistreat your child. But I try to be visible not just for my children, but for other Black children. They are not going to single your child out in an incident if you are visible and you also just want to make sure that they are doing things in the proper manner."

Proactive parenting. Proactive parents take the initiative to check on the children's performance in school *before* report cards are issued. Although the mothers did not wait to hear from the teachers, they found out the hard way that this does not always work. Lytia said she met with one teacher twice to check on her son's progress. "I talked to her about making sure that his average was decent and to make sure he should continue in the advanced placement courses for the new school year," she said.

Not only did the mothers talk to the teachers, they also talked to White parents. They wanted to know what kind of treatment they were receiving. Nia said her child and a friend's child were both struggling in the same class.

> "The parent would get a call from the teacher saying that her child is right on the bubble (borderline) for this and if he does A, B, and C, then he'll get it. I would call the teacher and the teacher wanted to know why I have to call so much. The teacher made me feel that I was an annoying parent, but my friend received reinforcements and helps and was told exactly what to study. So I found that frustrating. One time I had the parent to write a letter for my daughter to the teacher that was identical to the letter that she wrote for her son. Her son got help and I didn't hear back from the teacher for two weeks until I copied the letters to the principal. I heard from her the next day."

Other participants in this study have communicated with White parents to assess the discrepancies in the treatment they received. The mothers were baffled by how difficult it was for them to get questions answered while White parents received information, sometimes without an inquiry. The mothers agree with Crozier: the parent-teacher collaboration is critical to student success.

Battle Fatigue

The mothers knew their children were entitled to enjoy a quality education. Unfortunately, they could not rely on the school system to meet their children's needs. In fact, they have had to nurse their children's battle scars on a continuous basis and without any help from their schools. How do you build a child's self-esteem when they've been called a nigger, constantly neglected by their teachers, and isolated by their peers, all simply because they are African American? As a parent, how do you stay positive despite the battle fatigue?

For some mothers, it was a struggle just to recount these experiences during individual and group interviews. The mothers seethed, sighed, and wept. As Theresa said,

> "It should not be that I have to fight for everything, I mean every little thing. Now it is getting to the point where I am kind of tired. You know you just get to that point where you just get exhausted because it is a daily struggle. Daily. It is hard as a parent because you wonder every day when you send your kids to school— is that person going to be nice to your child? Are they going to be cordial? Can my child even feel that she can say she has to go to the bathroom and the teacher will tell her no but the next student will be able to go ahead? All

these things. I found with my daughter that it has broken her spirit."

Sheila agreed.

"It has been a terrible situation. It is such a struggle. Everyday you just wonder what is going to happen to my child. It is not a healthy place to be. I guess we really do not have any faith in the system. You know your child will get out and do fairly well, but you always wonder, 'Are you going to do as well as little Daniel over there?' He has not had to fight from our vantage point."

Barbara said, "My child is not as confident. It upsets me because I feel like they are messing with his future."

Theresa said, "I just get sick of the struggle. I feel like these teachers want to know why we want these things for our kids. We are just like everybody else."

Sheila said it was her job to help "gather enough self-esteem and enough joyous experiences to counteract what they do to our children."

If the mothers were battle fatigued, their children were demoralized and drained. Barbara said her son's "fire went out" as a result of his classroom experiences. The mothers were concerned about their children's emotional health, so they talked to them about how unfair life can be. They had to teach them how to deal with the racism that still exists in our society. In other words, they used these experiences as teachable moments to deliver lessons on some of life's harshest realities.

Hughes and Johnson say that "racial socialization practices are influenced both by indigenous family practices and by the nature of parents' daily experiences." They also influence children's identity development, racial pride, and overall well-being.

If students have a good racial identity and strong self-esteem, they are more likely to be productive and successful in school. Students who believe in their own ability to make superior grades in the classroom and on standardized tests can overcome even the most entrenched institutional racism found in school districts across the country.

Out of necessity, the mothers quickly established a routine following several racist incidents that occurred in the school. When the child came home with a complaint, the mothers worked on their children to build self-esteem. When teachers and administrators registered complaints about the children, the mothers listened with the understanding that racism had tainted the entire system. They could never be sure if the complaints were valid or not, so they tended to give their children the benefit of the doubt.

The mothers would ask their children, "How could this experience have been handled differently?" They wanted to show their children that they were not powerless or deficient.

The mothers continued to expect great things from their children. They refused to let them slow down in their school work. In fact, they were taught to work hard in the midst of obstacles.

"Do not let anyone dictate your destiny. The power to succeed lies within you. Never give up." Whether by word or deed or both, all mothers transmitted these messages to their children.

Interestingly, the mothers taught their children to respect teachers even when they felt they were being treated unfairly. Nia said her daughter's teacher mishandled a situation involving the school's Destination Imagination project, and the team was disqualified because of it—to the great disappointment of all involved. It would have been easy to blame the teacher, but Nia said,

> "I don't think my daughter should have disrespect for her teachers and that was not something she learned from me. I talked to her about going after what you want and getting it no matter who discourages you from that. We speak respectfully in front of our children about the teachers and we tell them that life isn't always easy, but you make the best out of whatever you get. Because those are life's lessons, to teach them that a person has problems does not equip them, and to teach them to make excuses does not equip them, even though they are there and they are real. But for me to teach them how to overcome every obstacle is priceless."

Chapter 8: Strategies to Educate All Children

It has been my sincere desire to give voice to the concerns of middle-income African American mothers regarding the achievement gap between African American students and other groups. The achievement gap, which has been studied from an institutional level, has focused on the plight of low-income, underserved urban students. This study may be the first to look at the achievement gap from the perspective of middle-income African American mothers whose children attend affluent, predominately White suburban schools. Some of the parents in the study have advanced degrees, and all have given their children the gift of cultural capital.

As we have heard from the mothers, the unfortunate reality of education in some suburban communities is that race continues to be a factor in educating African American children. The students have endured many uncomfortable, hurtful, and stigmatizing experiences in their classrooms. Instead of focusing on the curriculum and social experience, the mothers have had to fight for basic equity—in teacher-parent communication, access to advanced placement and preparatory classes, and fairness in disciplinary practices.

General Recommendations

The following are general recommendations based on the findings of this study:

1. School districts should commit to implementing a comprehensive curriculum that provides a fair and balanced view of how all races contributed to the formation of this country. The mothers in this study all

said that the teachers failed to teach history with racial sensitivity or a balanced approach to cultural diversity. Implementing this practice can foster a caring environment of cultural acceptance for African American students in the classrooms.

2. Policies regarding cultural diversity and sensitivity should be reevaluated systemically. We must now go beyond rhetoric and mere tolerance to the implementation of equity and justice for all students. The participants in this study were concerned about teachers seeing African American students through the lens of White middle-class privilege without regard to the specific needs of students of color.

3. Educators should deal with their low expectations of African American students. Our children are just as capable of academic achievement as any other group. As teachers begin to understand and learn how to work with students' different learning styles, we will see a narrowing of the achievement gap.

4. The faculty should reflect the diversity of the student population. From kindergarten to 12th grade and beyond, students need to see and interact with a culturally diverse professional community. A diverse faculty and administrative staff will lead to improved relationships and communication with parents, a more engaging curriculum, and overall, a more accepting school climate of cultural and racial differences.

5. Teacher preparation programs should incorporate cultural sensitivity and diversity training. Teachers should be prepared to work with a diverse population upon entering the classroom. Stereotypes, learning styles, and managing a racially diverse classroom should be addressed.

6. Educators should develop a school-wide support system for students of color to facilitate a sense of belonging. The mothers were concerned about their children's emotional well-being because no attempt had been made by teachers to make them feel welcome and a part of the school community.

Implications for Future Research

The following suggestions for additional research are based on the findings from this study:

1. This study was conducted with six middle-income African American mothers with children in suburban schools. Since Hispanic students also suffer academically and socially in diverse classrooms, this study should be replicated with middle-income Hispanic parents.
2. It would be interesting to study the suburban school experience from the perspective of middle-income African American students—specifically, their interactions with White teachers and peers.
3. This study examined the experiences of African American students in junior high school. It would be interesting to examine the elementary school experience as well.
4. It would be beneficial to compare and contrast the parents' perceptions relating to elementary and junior high experiences.
5. The children in this study all qualified for advance placement courses based on their standardized test scores. These students should be studied over an extended period of time to observe their level of academic attainment.

There is valuable knowledge to be gained from the narratives of the mothers. It is my sincere desire that educators will hear their voices and address their concerns, which in turn could lead to the narrowing of the achievement gap. African American mothers are a valuable resource. They know their children's strengths and weaknesses, and their opinions should not be discounted. They should not be considered "difficult" because they want to work with teachers. As their children's first teachers, African American mothers have a unique insight into educating children of color. To ignore them is to toss aside a rich body of knowledge that could turn things around for these children and other groups in the classroom.

I've had one urgent goal in mind from the beginning of this project and that has been to improve the experiences of African American students. Throughout the life of this project, there have been many challenges, including publishers who referred to this work in derogatory terms (which was very offensive to me). I persevered despite the challenges. Improving the treatment of African American students has been a driving force in the completion of this work. Countless parents and students have come to my office in tears, asking me to help them get through the school system. I've served as a mediator between the school system and Black families. It takes a village to raise a child, and there are peacemakers who must bring the warring factions of the village together.

The village (or suburb) should be child-centered. The child's well-being should be the primary concern of any community. *All* children should be treated equally and with respect. So in the spirit of the African proverb, the suburban village must aggressively work to improve the education of students, including African Americans.

Every aspect of the village should be a community of learning. Responsibilities should be shared by educators, parents, and students. Defour calls this a "Professional

Learning Community" (PLC). Teacher-parent partnerships are encouraged by the PLC's. PLC members share a vision, work and learn collaboratively, observe other classrooms, and participate in shared decision making. The benefits of the PLC include reduced isolation of teachers, better informed and committed teachers, and academic gains for students.

Educators, parents, and students must take an active role in creating a quality education for all children. It is important to develop healthy relationships to enhance their educational experiences. Relationships should be developed between parent and student, student and teacher, and educator and parent. These relationships must intertwine to achieve the desired outcomes.

Communication must flow freely to facilitate positive relationships between teachers and parents. They must feel comfortable enough with each other to discuss the challenges and progress of students. It would be helpful if teachers reached out to parents to *prevent* potential problems. For example, if a student is missing assignments or if grades are lower than the norm, the parent should be notified as soon as possible *before* the end of the grading cycle to give the parent an opportunity to address the situation with the student.

What Teachers Must Do

Educators often blame African American children and their families for the achievement gap. This is a classic case of blaming the victim for his own plight.

Needless to say, district-wide policy changes must be made to promote inclusivity of all cultures at every level of the school experience. Policy change is beyond the scope of this study; however, there are many practical things educators can do to help reach all children.

Save Our Children
The Struggle between Black Families and Schools

1. Connect with students. Build rapport and develop relationships that encompass an understanding of the diverse needs, strengths, and weaknesses of each student.
2. Validate students. Accept students for who they are. Contribute to the students' sense of value and self worth. Students need to hear that it is okay to be yourself.
3. Come to terms with your own biases. Self-evaluation is uncomfortable yet necessary. The question must be raised: does your philosophy of education or your background hinder you from providing the best education possible to each and every student?
4. Seize opportunities to incorporate cultural diversity into the classroom. Become aware of holidays, traditions, and cultural events, and incorporate examples throughout the curriculum.
5. Motivate students in order to provide an engaging, safe learning environment. Work to develop the potential of each student that enters the classroom door. Many of the students whose parents participated in this study have been accepted into Ivy League colleges and have attained great accomplishments.
6. Take the initiative to research and implement best practices for educating African American youth. In the words of Rita Dunn, "If children do not learn the way we teach, we must learn to teach the way they learn."

What Parents Must Do

The possibilities for educating children in this day and age are endless. Parents can enroll their children in private schools, take advantage of vouchers or school choice, or home school their children. Reputable public schools will always be a viable option. Although our laws support an equitable educational experience for African American students in public schools, parents must continue to be guarded and protect their vested interests (their prized possessions, their children) in the school system.

The following recommendations are offered to parents to help them take control of their children's education:

1. Share the wealth of knowledge about your children with teachers. In *From Roots to Wings: Successful Parenting African American Style*, Dr. Young says that parents have a wealth of knowledge about what works and what doesn't work with their children. Teachers can use this knowledge to begin meeting the needs of their students.
2. Instill a love of learning in your children. Emphasize the value of education and the benefits associated with a quality education.
3. Create a stimulating, culturally enriching environment in the home. Have your children participate in cultural events.
4. Teach your children how to make good academic and social decisions in the school setting.
5. Stay informed about school activities. Post the school calendar in a visible place at home and/or work. Become actively involved in the school system by joining parent-teacher associations, attending school board meetings, and participating in parenting workshops. Be aware of the laws and policies that impact your children's education.

What Students Must Do

Students enter school as empty vessels waiting to be filled with knowledge. When they are greeted with continual adversity at the hands of those commissioned to teach and nurture them, the vessel becomes broken or filled with confusion, doubt, anger, and low self-esteem. Students must, at all cost, resist developing a victim mentality. They should be equipped to strategically position themselves to receive every educational opportunity for success. The following strategies are recommended for students.

1. Assume leadership roles by participating in student activities, including academic and social clubs, organizations, and fine arts programs. Develop positive relationships with peers, teachers, and administrators to lessen feelings of isolation and strengthen a sense of belonging.

2. Set academic goals at the beginning of each school year.

3. Actively participate in class discussions.

4. Develop good study habits. Be attentive in class and take notes. If needed, get tutoring to enhance skills, and offer to tutor students who may be experiencing difficulties.

5. Resist negative peer pressure. Following the rules is critical to achieving success in school.

6. Seek to find your true identity in the midst of a culturally challenging environment. Although you, as an African American, are in the minority physically, you do not have to be in the minority mentally. Explore your history, become aware of the contributions of African Americans to society, and strive to add to the legacy of high achievers.

7. Speak respectfully and assertively to teachers. If you are having difficulty understanding a concept, be courageous and ask questions.

Chapter 9: The Mothers' Plea to Educators

The mothers wanted to share a final message to their children's teachers, so I will honor their wishes and conclude this book with their plea. As Condi said,

> "This sounds very trite and kind of juvenile, but it's the teachers' loss. They are missing out on knowing some great kids. They are missing out on providing these kids with insight and experiences they will never forget. They are the losers.
>
> "I think this situation has prepared my daughter for what is likely to be a common experience in her future, and I think that she has grown in her ability to maintain her ethnic identity and pride and still exist in that system. She expresses pride when given opportunities to write about something. For instance, she had to learn a poem and the poem she picked was 'Still I Rise.'"

Nia said,

> "I just think it's terrible. I just can't imagine an adult who wouldn't want to plant a seed in any child to make them blossom and grow and be all that they can be. I just don't understand the rationale that would make you withhold from a child and not pour into them. I don't understand the mentality. Why would someone want to kill someone's desire to learn?"

However, giving the teachers the benefit of the doubt, that ignorance rather than maliciousness has governed their pedagogy and classroom management, I will close this book with direct communication from the mothers: a letter to educators. Prayerfully, every White educator and administrator who reads these words will receive them in the spirit they have been given. The mothers do not want to fight you, nor do they want to be perceived as difficult. They want to establish a fruitful partnership with you for the sake of their children.

Dear Educators,

The first step in resolving the achievement gap between African American students and other groups is for schools to acknowledge that our children are not to be blamed. Still, in 21st century America, our children are treated differently.

At every level, a commitment must be made to treat all children fairly, including African Americans. Until it is acknowledged that this is not always the case, no change will occur. And another generation will be forced to endure racism and discrimination. Haven't we as a nation moved beyond that? Let the bigotry end today, for the sake of our children, yours and ours.

Please don't assume that your African American students are mentally deficient or unable to handle the rigors of advanced placement and honors classes. Assess and test fairly before making a decision. Then communicate that decision to us, the parents. Give us options to help us bring our children up to speed if needed.

We have high expectations of our children. When we were growing up, we were taught that we had to be twice as good as Whites in order to succeed in America. Let's teach our children something even better—that they must perform to the best of their ability, they must challenge themselves to excel in your class, and they must value and be grateful for the excellent education you are providing.

We teach our students that self-worth is derived from accomplish-ment, behaving with character, and always striving to do your best. We believe these character traits empower our children to succeed academically. We have laid a strong foundation so that when they get to your class, they will do their best. You can challenge them like you would any other student. They can handle it. Not only will we support you at home, we will offer our services on a regular basis in your classroom. We know how important we are to the equation.

Contrary to what you may have heard, African American culture is rich. Like any culture, it has its positive and negative elements, but we strive to stress the positive at home. So allow our children their cultural identity. Seek to understand, not condemn. And please, do not attempt to mold them in your image.

We moved to this community because of its outstanding reputation in educating students. We want what every parent wants: equal access to a quality education for our children.

On behalf of all African American mothers with school aged children, we ask that you work with us, not against us. Let us work together to ensure our children's academic success.

Sincerely,

Condi, Nia, Lytia, Sheila, Barbara, Theresa

References

American heritage dictionary (2nd ed.). (1982). Boston: Houghton Mifflin.

Anderson, J. D. (1988). *The education of Blacks in the South 1860-1935*. Chapel Hill, NC: University of North Carolina Press.

Anderson, J. D. (1995). Literacy and education in the Black experience. In L. V. Gadsen & D. A. Wagner (Eds.), *Literacy among African-American youth: Issues in learning, teaching, and schooling* (pp. 19–37). Cressking, NJ: Hampton Press.

Anderson, J. D. (2004). The historical context for understanding the test score gap. *Journal of Public Management and Social Policy, 10*(1), 2–22.

Ansalone, G. (2001). Schooling, tracking, and inequality. *Journal of Children and Poverty, 7*(1), 33–47.

Balfanz, R. and Legters, N. (2004). *Locating the Dropout Crisis*. Baltimore: Johns Hopkins University.

Bandera, A. (1982). Self-efficacy: Mechanism in human agency. *American Psychologist, 37*(2), 122–147.

Bankston, C. & Caldas, S. (1996). Majority African American schools and social injustice: The influence of de facto segregation on academic achievement. *Social Forces, 75*(2), 535–556.

Blumberg, R. L. (1984). *Civil Rights: The 1960's struggle.* Boston: Twayne.

Bound, J. & Turner, S. (2002). Going to war and going to college: Did World War II and the G.I. Bill increase educational attainment for returning Veterans? *Journal of Labor and Economics, 20*, 784–815.

Carter, N. (2003). *Convergence or divergence: Alignment of standards, assessment, and issues of diversity.* Washington, DC: AACTE.

Carter, N. (2005). *Teaching all children: Making it work.* West Conshohocken, PA: Infinity.

Chapman, T. K. (2005). Peddling backwards: Reflections of Plessy and Brown in the Rockford Public School de jure desegregation efforts. *Race Ethnicity and Education, 8*(1), 29–44.

Clark, R. M. (1983). *Family life and school achievement: Why poor Black children succeed or fail.* Chicago: University of Chicago Press.

Cozzens, L. (1998). *Brown v. Board of Education. African American history.* Retrieved September 4, 2006, from <www.fledge.watson.org/~lisa/blackhistory/ early.civilrights/ brown.html>.

Crozier, G. (1996). Black parents and school relationships: A case study. *Educational Review, 48*(3), 253–267.

References

Crozier, G. (1999). Is it a case of "We know when we're not wanted"? The parents' perspective on parent-teacher roles and relationships. *Educational Research, 41*(3), 315–328.

Delgado-Gaitan, C. (1991). *Involving parents in the schools: A process of empowerment.* American Journal of Education, *100*(1) 20–46.

Delpit, L. (1995). *Other people's children.* New York: The New Press.

Denzin, N. K., & Lincoln, Y. S. (1994). *Handbook of qualitative research.* Thousand Oaks, CA: Sage.

Detlefsen, R. R. (1991). *Civil Rights under Reagan.* San Francisco: Institute for Contemporary Studies Press.

Drummond, K. V. & Stipek, D. (2004). Low-income parents' beliefs about their role in children's academic learning. *The Elementary School Journal, 104*(3), 197–213.

Editorial Projects in Education, "Diplomas Count 2008: School to College: Can State P–16 Councils Ease the Transition?" Special issue, *Education Week*, 27, no. 40 (2008).

Erlandson, D., Harris, E., Skipper, B., & Allen, S. (1993). *Doing naturalistic inquiry: A guide to methods.* Newbury Park, CA: Sage.

Ferguson, R. F. (2001). *A diagnostic analysis of Black and White GPA disparities in Shaker Heights, Ohio* (Brookings Papers on Education Policy: 2001). Washington, DC: Brookings Institution.

Flores, B., Teft-Cousin, P., & Diaz, E. (1990). Transforming deficit myths about learning, language, and culture. *Language Arts, 68*, 369–378.

Fritzberg, G. (2001). Less than equal: A former urban school teacher examines the causes of educational disadvantagement. *The Urban Review, 33*(2), 107–129.

Gardere, J. (1999). *Smart parenting for African Americans.* New York: Kensington.

Graybill, S. W. (1997). Questions of race and culture: How they relate to the classroom for African American students. *Clearinghouse, 70*(6), 311–318.

Greene, J.P. & Winters, M. (2005). Public High School Graduation and College Readiness: 1991-2002 (New York: Manhattan Institute for Policy Research.

Grossman, F. D. & Ancess, J. (2004). Narrowing the gap in affluent schools: Through collaborative action research, three suburban school districts are creatively confronting achievement differences. *Educational Leadership*, 70–73.

References

Gutman, M. L. & McLoyd, V. C. (2000). Parents' management of their children's education within the home, at school, and in the community: An examination of African American families living in poverty. *The Urban Review, 32*(1), 1–24.

Harris, L.C. (2004). *It all starts at home: 15 ways to put family first.* Grand Rapids: Fleming H. Revell.

Henderson-Cole, B. (2000). Organizational characteristics of schools that successfully serve low-income urban African American students. *Journal of Education for Students Placed At Risk, 5*(1&2), 77–91.

Hoy, A. (2000). *Changes in teacher efficacy during the early years of teaching.* Paper presented at the annual meeting of the American Education Research Association, New Orleans.

Hu, A. (1997). Education and race: The performance of minority students in affluent areas refutes the prevailing educational shibboleths. *National Review,* pp. 52–56.

Hughes, D. & Johnson, D. (2001). Correlates in children's experiences of parents' racial socialization behaviors. *Journal of Marriage and Family, 63,* 981–995.

Kuykendall, C. (2004). *From rage to hope: Strategies for reclaiming Black and Hispanic students.* Bloomington: Solution Tree.

Ladson-Billings, G. (1995). But that's just good teaching! The case for culturally relevant pedagogy. *Theory Into Practice, 34*(3), 159–165.

Ladson-Billings, G. (1998). Just what is critical race theory and what's it doing in a nice field like education? *International Journal of Qualitative Studies in Education, 11*(1), 7–24.

Lopez, G. R. (2001). The value of hard work: Lessons on parent involvement from an (im)migrant household. *Harvard Educational Review, 71,* 416–437.

Lott, B. (2003). Recognizing and welcoming the standpoint of low-income parents in public schools. *Journal of Educational and Psychological Consultation, 14*(1), 91–104.

Lynn, M. (1999). Toward critical race pedagogy: A research note. *Urban Education, 33*(5), 606–627.

Merriam, S. B. (1991). How research produces knowledge. In J. M. Peters & P. Jarvis (Eds.), *Adult education* (pp. 42–65). San Francisco: Jossey-Bass.

Merriam, S. B. (1998). *Qualitative research and case study applications in education.* San Francisco: Jossey-Bass.

Myers, L. M. (1997). *Civil rights and race relations in the post Reagan-Bush era.* Wesport: Praeger.

References

Neild, R.C. & Balfanz, R. (2001). *An Extreme Degree of Difficulty: The Educational Demographics of the Ninth Grade in Philadelphia.* Baltimore: Johns Hopkins University.

Nettles, M. T. & Perna, L. W. (1997). *The African American data book.* Fairfax, VA: Patterson Research Institute of the College Fund/UNCF.

Noguera, P. & Akom, A. (2002). Causes of the racial achievement gap all derive from unequal treatment: Disparities demystified. *The Nation, 270,* 22–29.

Oakes, J. (1995). Two cities' tracking and within-school segregation. *Teachers College Record, 96*(4), 681–690.

Office of Vocational and Adult Education. (2002). "High School Reading: Key Issue Brief." Washington, DC: U.S. Department of Education.

Ogbu, J.U. (2003). *Black American students in an affluent suburb: A study of academic disengagement.* Mahwah: Lawrence Erlbaum Associates.

Orfield, G., Frankenberg, E. D., & Lee, C. (2003). The resurgence of school segregation. *Educational Leadership, 60,* 16–20.

Orfield, G. & Lee, C. (2006). *Racial transformation and the changing nature of segregation.* Cambridge, MA: Harvard University, The Civil Rights Project.

Parker, G. M. & O'Conner, W. (1970). Racism in the schools: A response using laboratory training. *Training and Development Journal*, 27–32.

Patton, M. Q. (1990). *Qualitative evaluation and research methods*. Newbury Park, CA: Sage.

Payne, C. M. (2004). The whole United States is Southern!: Brown v. Board and the mystification of race. *The Journal of American History*, 83–91.

Poplin, M., & Weeres, L. (1992). *Voices from the inside: A report on schooling from inside the classroom*. Claremont, CA: Claremont Graduate School.

Richards, H. (1997). The teaching of Afrocentric values by African American parents. *The Western Journal of Black Studies, 21*(1), 42–50.

Rothman, R. (2001). Closing the achievement gap: How schools are making it happen. *Challenge Journal, 5*(2), 1–11.

Scheurich, J., Skrla, L., & Johnson, J. (2000). Thinking carefully about equity and accountability. *Phi Delta Kappan, 82*(4), 293–299.

Simpson, J. (2001). Segregated by subject: Racial differences in the factors influencing academic major between European Americans, Asian Americans, African, Hispanic, and Native Americans. *Journal of Higher Education, 72*, 63–90.

References

Spindler, G. D. (1963). *Education and culture: Anthropological approaches*. New York: Holt, Rinehart, & Winston.

Spring, J. (2002). *Conflict of interest in American education.* New York: McGraw Hill.

Stake, R. E. (1995). *The art of case study research.* Thousand Oaks, CA: Sage.

Tatum, B. D. (2004). Family life and school experience: Factors in the racial identity development of Black youth in White communities. *Journal of Social Issues, 60*(1), 117–135.

Thompson, G. L. (2003). No parent left behind: Strengthening ties between educators and African American parents/ guardians. *The Urban Review, 35*(1), 7–23.

U.S. Department of Education, National Center for Education Statistics. (2007) *The Nation's Report Card: Reading 2007* (NCES 2007-496). Washington, DC: U.S. Government Printing Office.

U.S. Department of Education, National Center for Education Statistics, "NAEP Data Explorer," Retrieved September 22, 2008 from http://nces.ed.gov/ nationsreportcard/nde/.

Vincent, C. (2001). Social class and parental agency. *Journal of Educational Policy, 16*(4), 347–364.

Walker, V. S. (2000). Valued segregated schools for African American children in the South. *Review of Educational Research, 70*, 253–286.

Young, J.C. (2006). *From roots to wings: Successful parenting African American Style.* Chicago: African American Images.

Zirkel, S. (2004). What will you think of me? Racial integration, peer relationships and achievement among White students and students of color. *Journal of Social Issues, 60*(1), 57–74.

Notes

_____

_____

_____

_____

_____

_____

_____

_____

_____

_____

_____

_____

_____

_____

_____

_____

_____

Notes

_____

_____

_____

_____

_____

_____

_____

_____

_____

_____

_____

_____

_____

_____

_____

_____

Notes

Notes

Notes

Notes

Notes

Notes

Notes

_____

_____

_____

_____

_____

_____

_____

_____

_____

_____

_____

_____

_____

_____

_____

_____

_____

_____

Notes

_____

_____

_____

_____

_____

_____

_____

_____

_____

_____

_____

_____

_____

_____

_____

_____

_____

_____

Notes

Notes

Notes

Notes

Notes

Notes